A Study of Remington's Smoot Patent & Number Four Revolvers

E. REMINGTON & SONS,

MANUFACTURERS OF

GUNS, RIFLES; REVOLVERS, RIFLE AND GUN BARRELS, MATERIAL, &c.

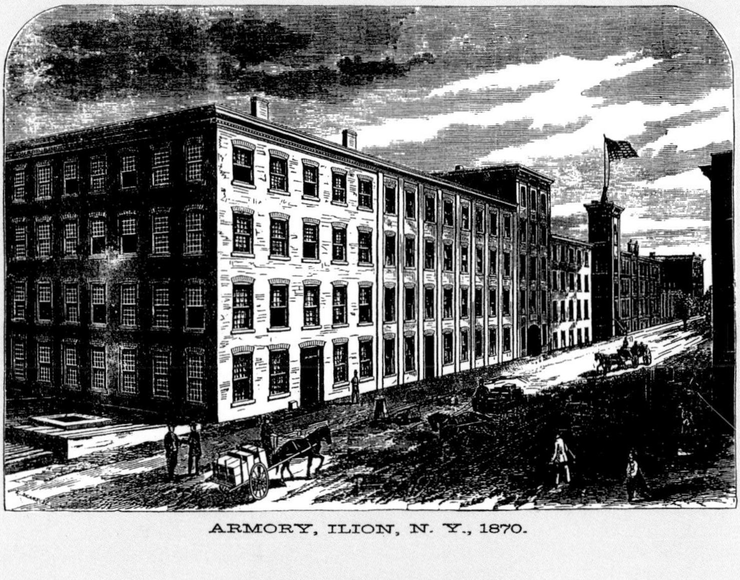

ARMORY, ILION, N. Y., 1870.

Harry J. Parker, Ph.D.
Ora Lee Parker, M.A.
Joan S. Reisch, Ph.D.

Armslore Press : 2003

First Edition

Printed and bound in South Korea

Library of Congress Catalog Card Number 2001098786

ISBN 1-882824-21-0

A fine collector arms volume from

ARMSLORE PRESS

division of Graphic Publishers

Post Office Box 10787
Santa Ana, California 92711-0787 USA
1-800-4 YOUR BOOK

Foreword

by Roy M. Marcot

The history of the Remington company mirrors the history of the United States. Indeed, the company that bears the founder's name is one of the oldest manufacturers in this country still making its original product: firearms. Established by Eliphalet Remington II in 1816, the company has gone through several name changes: from *Remingtons* (1816 to 1828), to *E. Remington & Son* (1828 to 1856), to *E. Remington & Sons* (1856 to 1888), to *Remington Arms Company* (1888 to 1911), to *Remington Arms and Ammunition Company* (1912 to 1916), to *Remington Arms Union Metallic Cartridge Company* (1916 to 1920), and to *Remington Arms Company, Inc.* (1920 to present).

This company most often manufactured sporting arms and ammunition for the public, including pistols, carbines, rifles, and shotguns. But in times of war the Remington company stepped forward to make arms and munitions for America's fighting forces, including activity in the American Civil War, the Spanish-American War, World Wars I and II, the Korean War, and the War in Viet Nam. As it was, Remington provided more than half the arms and ammunition used by the Allies in "the War to End all Wars"—World War I—and twenty years later supplied more than half the small arms ammunition used by all of the Allied Forces combined in World War II. It is enough to say that Remington was there when our country needed her most.

Remington is best known in times of peace and prosperity for making sporting arms for hunting, target shooting, and self-protection. Remington barrels were affixed to flintlock and percussion rifles fabricated by hundreds of gunmakers throughout the Americas from the 1820s through the 1850s. Those rifles protected families as they journeyed west into the new frontier, and brought meat to the settlers' tables. Remington revolvers and pocket pistols were popular in the 1860s, '70s, and '80s as a means of protection in lawless towns throughout the country. Remington single- and double-barrel shotguns were prized by wing shooters and trap shooters from the 1870s through the turn of the century. Remington rolling block rifles, Hepburn single-shot rifles, Keene and Lee sporting rifles were used by hunters and target shooters alike. And in the later half of the twentieth century, well-made Remington Model 870 pump shotguns, Model 1100 shotguns, and Model 700 rifles dominated the sporting market.

Over the past fifty years, nearly twenty informative and authoritative books have been written on Remington firearms. All, it appears, have increased the collecting and shooting interest in Remington. But one area has been neglected up until now: that of the Smoot Patent No. 1, No. 2, and No. 3 revolvers, and the No. 4 revolvers. Author Harry Parker wrote about these pocket revolvers in arms magazines during the mid-1970s, but several generations of collectors have grown up not having read Dr. Parker's words. Now, nearly thirty years later, with the benefit of many more years' study of existing specimens, Dr. Parker and his wife and associate have produced this epic volume.

Readers will appreciate the authors' dedication, and the meticulous manner in which they undertook this endeavor. They have successfully combined in one volume a biography of the revolvers' inventor, with a concise history of E. Remington & Sons, with an engineer's approach to the study of the manufacturing process of the guns. All in all, this book is a welcome addition to the Remington bookshelf, and a classic study that will remain unchallenged for decades to come.

Roy Marcot
Tucson, Arizona
March, 2003

Publisher's note: *A respected firearms researcher, historian, and writer, Roy Marcot is the author of* Spencer Repeating Firearms, Hiram Berdan—Chief of Sharpshooters, *and* Remington—America's Oldest Gunmaker, *as well as numerous articles on firearms and related subjects. Since 1991 he has been the editor of the* RSA Journal, *a quarterly publication of the Remington Society of America.*

Contents

Foreword, *by Roy M. Marcot* iii

Biography of William S. Smoot vii

Introduction xiii

I. No. 1 Smoot Patent Revolvers 17

Color Plates of Smoot Patent and No. 4 Revolvers 41-48

II. No. 2 Smoot Patent Revolvers 53

III. No. 3 Smoot Patent Revolvers 67

IV. No. 4 New Model Revolvers 93

Table of Serial Number Ranges, Production, Finishes, Grip Materials,
and Calibers for the three Smoot Patent and the No. 4 Revolvers 108

Epilogue 109

The Firearms Patents of William Sydney Smoot 110

Bibliography 115

Acknowledgments 117

Index 119

Remington
SINCE 1816

Property of AT&T Archives. Reprinted with permission of AT&T.

WILLIAM SYDNEY SMOOT
1845-1886

William S. Smoot

William Sydney Smoot was one of America's genuine Industrial Age geniuses. He had more than a dozen firearms patents to his credit, and held high-level positions with E. Remington & Sons from 1871 through the early 1880s. A successful revolver model made by Remington bears his name. He served as president of the burgeoning Western Electric Company, a unit of the American Bell Telephone Company. It is a wonder, then, that the man is so little-known today.

Despite a distinguished arms-making career, his name is barely mentioned in any of the standard Remington histories. They offer virtually no biographical or genealogical information. Hatch[1] doesn't even cite W.S. Smoot. That Smoot was successful is undisputed. Perhaps the fact that his life was cut short only one month before his forty-first birthday accounts, in part, for his historical anonymity. Feeling that Smoot was a man worth knowing, Newman[2] traced the genealogy of the Smoot family, and the authors of this volume set out to re-discover William Sydney Smoot.

William was born in Norfolk, Virginia on 12 March 1845, the son of a career U.S. Naval officer. His early years were spent in the Washington, D.C. area. According to naval records[3,4] his father, Joseph E. Smoot, was a captain in the U.S. Navy, although he was frequently referred to as "admiral." Captain Smoot was "aggrieved" by the Federal Act of 1855, the stated purpose of which was "to improve the efficiency of the U.S. Navy." The impact of that act on the upper level naval officers corps was reported in the minutes of the *Congressional Globe*[5] (now known as the *Congressional Record*). In his papers[6] Samuel Francis DuPont of the renowned DuPont de Nemours family, an active advocate of reform and also a career naval officer, related his advocacy of reform and of professionalizing the navy. DuPont was particularly involved with the Naval Efficiency Board, and his activities generated voluminous correspondence. Ultimately, the resultant turmoil affected both Captain Joseph Smoot and his son William Sydney.

During the Civil War W.S. Smoot served as a lieutenant in the First Maryland Infantry (Volunteer) as part of the Union forces (23 December 1863 to 1 July 1864). From 29 January 1864 he served as a second lieutenant in the U.S. Ordnance Department[7], was awarded a brevet[8] to first lieutenant for faithful and meritorious service on 13 March 1864[9], and received a promotion to full first lieutenant on 1 March 1867. Perhaps of more importance is that Lieutenant Smoot spent the last part of the Civil War as an ordnance officer at Springfield Armory[10], a position that undoubtedly prepared him for his later responsibilities with E. Remington & Sons.

William S. Smoot resigned his army commission on 31 December 1870, and began his employment at Remington in 1871. An *R.G. Dun Report*[11] stated that Smoot "Receives salary of $3,000-$4,000 a year, pays promptly, is Superintendent in the Cartridge Department." He rose to become superintendent of the armory later that same year. However, both Schulz[12] and Smith[13] indicated that J.W. Clough was superintendent until 1877, whereupon Smoot took over. Karr & Karr[14] assign ten lines, or approximately one hundred words, to Smoot's history and experience before and during his Remington tenure. The same source indicates that Smoot became a trustee for the firm, before leaving it in 1885, but no confirmation of his trustee role or 1885 termination date has been found elsewhere.

While still an Army ordnance officer Smoot married Miss Mary Bangs, nineteen years of age, on 25 April 1866 in Brookline, Massachusetts. The Smoots settled in the Boston area. Over the subsequent years their union produced seven children: William Sydney, Jr. (b. 1868), Sarah Marquard (b. 1869), Anna Titcomb (b. 1872), Joseph Edward (b. 1873), Charles Head (b. 1878), Mary (b. 1880), and Margaret (b. 1885).

Apparently at some point Smoot became disenchanted with Remington management, and began looking for other opportunities. Although the circumstances surrounding his departure from Remington remain unknown, the year has been confirmed as 1883. An 1883 *R.G. Dun Report* noted that he had "Sold everything here and gone west, circumstances not known. Said to be going into the cattle business."[15] It is likely that over the years Smoot had established numerous business and investment relationships. Not only did he invest a considerable amount of his own money in the cattle enterprise[16], but he knew monied individuals who were interested in doing the same.

How, then, did William Sydney Smoot move from a military career, to one in management with the Remington company, to part ownership of a Montana cattle ranch, to the presidency of Western Electric Company? The first three we have traced. But to understand Smoot's affiliation with Western Electric, we need to know a bit about that firm's history.

In 1869 George Shawk and Enos Barton formed a company in Cleveland, Ohio, to manufacture fire and burglar alarms as well as other electrical devices. One source has referred to it as an "acorn of enterprise."[17] One of the firm's first customers was Elisha Gray, a physics professor at Oberlin College. Both Gray and Enos Barton foresaw the future of the then-developing electrical age. George Shawk did not, and his interest was acquired by Elisha Gray.

Both Gray and Barton were acquainted with General Anson Stager, who had been Chief of U.S. Military Telegraphers during the Civil War. Stager invested money in the nascent company, eventually purchasing a fifty percent interest in it.

The yellow brick Victorian home of Remington Armory Superintendent William S. Smoot and family, on West Street in Ilion, New York. Photograph probably was taken during the 1880s. *Courtesy the Herkimer County (NY) Historical Society*

Thus he became not only a partner, but afterward its president. During his tenure the company was renamed Western Electric and moved to Chicago, Illinois.

Stager sought inventions and new products for his company. Mechanical and electrical components to facilitate telegraphy and data transmission were priorities. Stager also indicated that he was looking for duplicate copying capability. Enos Barton was asked to examine typewriter manufacturing in the United States, which led him to E. Remington & Sons. Barton and Stager then contracted with W.S. Smoot to purchase the company's typewriter line.[18] After the sale, Remington ended typewriter production.

In 1881 General Stager, as president of Western Electric, signed an agreement whereby his firm was to become the manufacturing component of the American Bell Telephone Company. However he was forced to resign his position due to ill health in 1885, and died soon afterward. Upon Stager's death William Sydney Smoot was named president of Western Electric Company.

Ironically, Smoot's tenure as president of Western Electric was even more short-lived than Stager's. Less than one year later he died from a "sudden illness" that was described as "untimely" and "shocking" by the Ilion *Citizen*.[19] It seems that Smoot's physicians diagnosed him as having nothing more than a severe cold. But after ten days he showed unmistakable signs of typhoid fever, from which he did not recover.[20] Both his residence and place of death were in Evanston, Illinois; howev-

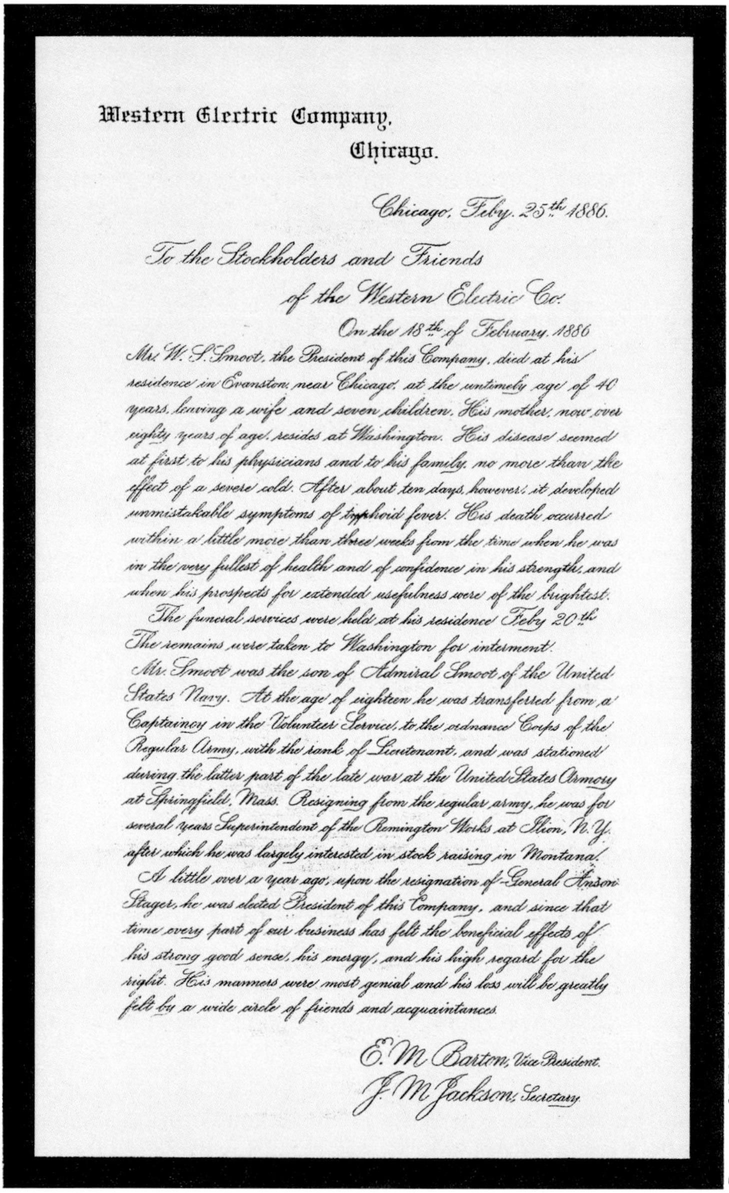

Western Electric Company,
Chicago.

Chicago, Feby. 25th 1886.

To the Stockholders and Friends
of the Western Electric Co.

On the 18th of February, 1886 Mr. W. S. Smoot, the President of this Company, died at his residence in Evanston, near Chicago, at the untimely age of 40 years, leaving a wife and seven children. His mother, now over eighty years of age, resides at Washington. His disease seemed at first to his physicians and to his family, no more than the effect of a severe cold. After about ten days, however, it developed unmistakable symptoms of typhoid fever. His death occurred within a little more than three weeks from the time when he was in the very fullest of health and of confidence in his strength, and when his prospects for extended usefulness were of the brightest.

The funeral services were held at his residence Feby 20th. The remains were taken to Washington for interment.

Mr. Smoot was the son of Admiral Smoot of the United States Navy. At the age of eighteen he was transferred from a Captaincy in the Volunteer Service, to the ordnance Corps of the Regular Army, with the rank of Lieutenant, and was stationed during the latter part of the late war at the United States Armory at Springfield, Mass. Resigning from the regular army, he was for several years Superintendent of the Remington Works at Ilion, N.Y. after which he was largely interested in stock raising in Montana.

A little over a year ago, upon the resignation of General Anson Stager, he was elected President of this Company, and since that time every part of our business has felt the beneficial effects of his strong good sense, his energy, and his high regard for the right. His manners were most genial and his loss will be greatly felt by a wide circle of friends and acquaintances.

E. M. Barton, Vice President.
J. M. Jackson, Secretary.

er, Smoot's estate was probated in Suffolk County, Massachusetts, as members of his family had property in the Boston area. Interment was in Washington, D.C.

Because of his long tenure and executive positions with the Remington company and Western Electric, one might expect to find extensive coverage of him in the local press. But that is not the case. Examination of representative issues of the Ilion *Citizen* between 1871 and 1885 reveals little mention of

Smoot's achievements. Occasionally his receipt of a patent was noted, but little more, which is curious inasmuch as he was granted over a dozen patents beginning when he was in ordnance service. Their variety is noteworthy, too: from metallic cartridges to an extractor for a breechloading arm; a cartridge primer; from a magazine firearm, to a machine gun, to a trowel bayonet. He kept up lively correspondence with the U.S. Patent Office, as well, for clarification of the details he was claiming. In addition, his duties at Remington took him to Europe, where he met many foreign dignitaries who were contracting for arms purchases with the company. Smoot also was known to have traveled to and from the Boston area frequently, and to the West, as well as back and forth to Ilion.

But despite his wide-ranging accomplishments, the *Citizen* consistently allotted more column inches to Smoot's shooting skills at the Ilion Rifle Club than to his business achievements. Another source likewise related only that "Lieutenant Smoot was among the top scorers on Ilion's new range."[21] Others, writing on the history of Remington firearms, followed the *Citizen*'s lead and virtually omitted substantive mention of Smoot.[22] The firearms literature of today has done him little more justice. All of the foregoing seems ironically incompatible with the role played on history's broad stage by William Sydney Smoot. He was indeed a man worth knowing, as the following story proves.

Notes:

1. Alden Hatch, *Remington Arms in American History*, p. 6.
2. Harry W. Newman, *The Smoots of Maryland and Virginia*, pp. 32, 41.
3. File of Captain Joseph E. Smoot, in *Records of Officers* (microfilm publication M330, rolls 2-7), National Archives, Washington, D.C.
4. Edward W. Callahan, *List of Officers of the U.S. Navy and Marine Corps from 1775 to 1900*, p. 510.
5. *The Congressional Globe*, Thirty-third Congress, 2nd Session, February 2, 12-14, 23, 26-28, March 1, 1855.
6. Papers of Samuel F. DuPont (1806-1865), Winterthur manuscripts, group 9, in the Hugley Museum, Wilmington, DE.
7. Francis B. Heitman, *Historical Register and Dictionary of the United States Army, From Its Organization September 29, 1798 to March 2, 1903* (Volume I), p. 905.
8. A *brevet* is a commission giving a military officer higher nominal rank but not the correspondingly higher pay scale.
9. Heitman, page 905.
10. Obituary of William S. Smoot, published 25 February 1886 for the "Stockholders and Friends" of Western Electric Company (hereafter referred to as "*Smoot Obituary*").
11. *R.G. Dun Report*, Vol. I, 8 February 1871, p. 163.
12. Warren E. Schulz, *Ilion—The Town Remington Made*, p. 91.
13. Arthur T. Smith, *Papers Read Before the Herkimer County Historical Society, New York, 1896-1898*, p. 84.
14. Charles L. Karr, Jr. and Carroll R. Karr, *Remington Handguns,* p. 78.
15. *R.G. Dun Report*, Vol. XV, 3 August 1883, p. 10.
16. The *Smoot Obituary* states that his cattle interests were in Montana.
17. Albert B. Iardella, *Western Electric and the Bell System, a Survey of Service*, p. 27.
18. Stephen B. Adams and Orville R. Butler, *Manufacturing the Future: A Survey of Western Electric*, pp. 33-34.
19. Ilion and Herkimer (New York) *Citizen*, Vol. II, No. 24, 26 February 1886.
20. *Smoot Obituary.*
21. *R.G. Dun Report*, Vol. 115, 1883, p. 163.
22. Smith, p. 84.

ELIPHALET REMINGTON II
FOUNDER OF E. REMINGTON & SONS
OCTOBER 28, 1793 – JULY 12, 1861

Introduction

Remington gun lore tells the story of how on a crisp October morning in 1816 a young man raised a new rifle to his shoulder, took aim, and fired. The occasion was a shooting match held at Crane's Corners, a short distance from his family's home in Litchfield, New York. Continuing, the story relates that after the young man won second place that day, a number of fellow contestants admired his gun, hefted it, took aim along its long, slender barrel–and asked where he got one that shot so straight. "Made it myself," came the answer with well-deserved pride, and when asked what he would charge to make another barrel like it he replied, "ten dollars."

However it actually came about, we do know that twenty-three-year-old Eliphalet Remington II, or "Lite" as he was called, did in fact begin hand-making iron rifle barrels, probably using the tools at the forge where his father built plows and other agricultural implements. It is likely that at first he would have carried his barrels the ten or so miles to Utica to be bored out and rifled by a local gunsmith, yet before long he either made or bought the machinery to do those operations himself. However humble was the start of Eliphalet Remington's gun barrel business, it marked the beginning of an arms-making dynasty that eventually became renowned the world over as E. Remington & Sons.

In early nineteenth century America, guns were as much a family necessity as automobiles are in today's society. Hunting birds and other small game put food on the family table. Guns also protected settlers from attack by wild animals, or by equally-wild Indians. Muskets for state militias had been manufactured by private contractors in Bridgeport, Connecticut since the middle 1700s, and the two government arsenals at Springfield, Massachusetts and Harpers Ferry, Virginia began turning out military longarms during 1795 and 1800, respectively. But there were very few private firms engaged in the production of firearms for the civilian populace. Men who could afford fine arms imported them from the famed European arms-making capitals of London, Paris, and Liége. Others had their rifles made by individual local gunsmiths, who often doubled as blacksmiths. They generally fitted imported locks, barrels, and hardware—"furniture," the latter was called—onto stocks they made themselves.

Word traveled fast that young Eliphalet Remington could supply any type of gun barrel requested, and orders began pouring in. It is said that by the middle

1820s the fledgling company was shipping two to three hundred hand-finished barrels per year. By the 1840s Remington-made barrels dominated the trade.

In 1828 Lite bought one hundred acres of land bordering the south bank of the Mohawk River. There he put up a stone drop forge, and the new village of Ilion soon grew up around it. In 1837 Philo Remington, the oldest of Eliphalet's sons, came of age and entered his father's business. One of Philo's earliest contributions to the firm—now called E. Remington & Son—was an improvement to the barrel straightening process. Samuel joined the company in 1839 and was followed by Eliphalet III in 1849. But it wasn't until 1856 that the firm's name was changed to E. Remington & Sons.

The company's first government arms contract came in 1845. War with Mexico was imminent, with the result that the United States government awarded John Griffiths of Cincinnati a contract to manufacture 5,000 Model 1841 "Mississippi" rifles on the pattern of those made at the Harpers Ferry Armory. When Griffiths failed to deliver any rifles Remington stepped in, purchased the contract, and shipped all 5,000. He received a contract for 1,000 Jenks carbines with Maynard tape primer mechanisms later that same year, and other contracts soon followed, necessitating almost continual armory expansion and additions even before the Civil War.

With war clouds again on the horizon in 1861, U.S. Secretary of War Edwin M. Stanton inquired of Remington, "How many guns can you make for us?" The company rapidly began a program of enlarging its arms-making facilities, and soon after Remington was turning out new rifles, bayonets, and revolvers by the thousands, in addition to altering old flintlock government muskets to the percussion system. As Union troops often had to make coffee in the field, the firm even fitted some of their carbines with integral coffee grinders in their buttstocks.

Despite his Yankee hardiness, the constant days and nights of overwork to meet wartime production demands cost Eliphalet Remington dearly. That July, he

The Armory of E. Remington & Sons.

collapsed and died. The three Remington sons now began carrying on their father's work.

With Civil War arms production at an all-time high in 1864, five new buildings were constructed and filled with new machinery to ensure the firm's armory would remain at peak capacity. The plant also had to expand its workforce to keep pace with the backlog of government arms orders.

Then, on April 9th, 1865, at a sleepy crossroads called Appomattox Court House, Confederate General Robert E. Lee surrendered his Army of Northern Virginia to Union General Ulysses S. Grant, and the Civil War passed into history. Just two days later the huge Remington armory at Ilion stood silent. No smoke rose from its massive chimneys, no workers labored amid the din of machinery, no sounds of industry rang out. The government had quickly cancelled its arms contracts, and there were no more orders to be filled.

For most of the country the end of the Civil War was cause for celebration. For the country's arms-makers, however, the cease-fire was nothing short of traumatic. For four years production lines had run around the clock, supplying arms and ammunition for the war effort. Now, to cope with America's postwar economic downturn, gun makers had to convert to the manufacture of products for the civilian market. To make things worse, by the early 1870s the country was in the grip of a depression, and mere survival became a formidable challenge for those whose livelihood depended on the production and sale of firearms.

But there was reason for optimism. Although the Civil War left many former soldiers rootless and many families seeking to begin a new life, the Mexican War had granted much new territory to the country. The United States was finally beginning to realize its goal of Manifest Destiny. Expanding the nation into the vast and uncharted lands west of the Sabine River stimulated the need for weapons of personal protection as well as of survival. Repeating rifles and pistols were what was needed. The arms companies like Remington, Colt, Spencer, and Sharps recognized opportunity when they saw it.

And a man named William Sydney Smoot would receive the plaudits for one of the most successful new revolver designs of that era. He would also benefit from the Remington company's experience with patent laws.

In 1888 E. Remington & Sons was acquired by Hartley & Graham, owners of the Union Metallic Cartridge Company. E. Remington & Sons was reorganized and renamed the Remington Arms Company. In 1911 the two companies merged to become Remington–UMC.

In 1914 war once again dominated Remington arms production, resulting in expansion of the Ilion facilities with buildings on both sides of Main Street connected by overhead bridges, and the installation of new machinery. By the time the Armistice ending World War I was signed on November 11, 1918, Remington had supplied sixty-nine percent of the rifles and small arms manufactured for U.S. troops, and more than fifty percent of the ammunition expended by the U.S. and her allies.

In order to make better use of its facilities after the war, Remington branched into new fields. This was not the company's first non-gun making venture. As far back in 1873 it had begun making Remington typewriters and sewing machines. However, as the arms business improved, the typewriter business was sold. It later became Remington Rand, and then Sperry Rand. After World War I, Remington again diversified, and by 1920 the company was manufacturing cutlery and cash registers.

In the wake of financial problems brought on by the 1929 Depression, the E.I. DuPont de Nemours & Co. purchased a sixty percent share of the company in 1933. There followed an ambitious expansion program, including the acquisition of the Chamberlain Trap & Target Company, the Peters Cartridge Company in Ohio, and the Parker Shotgun Company in Connecticut. In 1936 it purchased a sporting ammunition plant in Brazil, and in 1940 began collaborating with the U.S. government to expand ammunition production. By the close of World War II, five new plants in Utah, Missouri, Colorado, and New England were in operation.

Since the Second World War Remington has continued to expand, introducing a variety of new products including firearms, targets, and ammunition. In 1993 the corporation's assets were acquired by Clayton, Dubilier and Rice, and in 1997 the company moved to new corporate headquarters in Madison, North Carolina. A new firearms plant was opened in Mayfield, Kentucky in 1997, the first new site since the arms plant in Bridgeport, Connecticut was built in 1915.

Beginning in 1935 the Remington Arms Company became active in the field of wildlife conservation, and has actively promoted scientific game management programs since. In 1956 the company established Remington Farms, near Chestertown, Maryland. The facility is utilized for hunting and related conference functions, with its primary mission being the restoration of wildlife and the demonstration of wildlife conservation techniques.

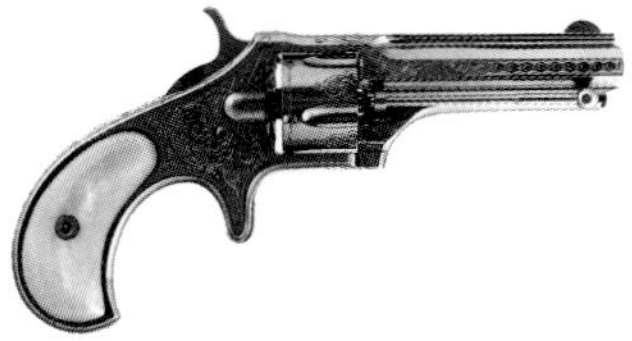

Chapter I

Remington Number 1 (Smoot's Patent) New Model Revolver

A post Civil War attempt by E. Remington & Sons to create a market for percussion revolvers, particularly those converted to fire the new, self-contained metallic cartridges, proved unsuccessful. In his book *Remington Arms in American History*[1], Alden Hatch relates how the origin and establishment of the Union Metallic Cartridge Company (UMC) in 1867 energized the development and sale of cartridge long guns, including the Remington Rolling-Block rifle, which found favor principally in foreign countries. UMC provided cartridge development for Remington until 1871, when the company established its own cartridge works in Ilion. Hatch's book offers a thorough review of the Remington company's management history, its involvements, and the part it played in international arms politics. The author describes the years between 1870 and 1880 as the "gay decade," and Ilion, New York as the "boom town on the Erie." He interpreted those times in a genteel manner, using the term "golden age." That view was influenced by the arms contracts that stimulated factory building and company expansion. Overarching all was Remington's attention to high moral and fiscal standards, embodied in the company's focus on scientific and mechanical developments. This idyllic depiction of Ilion was in sharp contrast to the ongoing depression throughout much of the rest of the country. Nevertheless, despite a lack of success with percussion-to-cartridge conversion revolvers, Remington went forward with its development of modern revolving-cylinder handguns.

E. Remington & Sons had begun offering small revolvers and pistols for sale in the late 1850s. Then, at the onset of the Civil War, Remington's Fordyce Beals created large- and medium-frame revolvers known as the .44 caliber "Army" and .36 caliber "Navy" models, that were intended for military use. Firearms inventor Joseph Rider developed the double-action revolver for Remington, and William Elliot created single- and multiple-shot pistols. Up to the year 1870 Remington offered Rider's Vest Pocket pistols, Elliot's ring-trigger pistols, New Model Belt revolvers (single and double action), New Model Police and New Model pocket revolvers, Split Breech pistols, walking-cane rifles, and small frame revolving rifles (initially as percussion, but later made as cartridge models).

Other arms-making companies, such as Colt, Sharps, and H. Deringer,

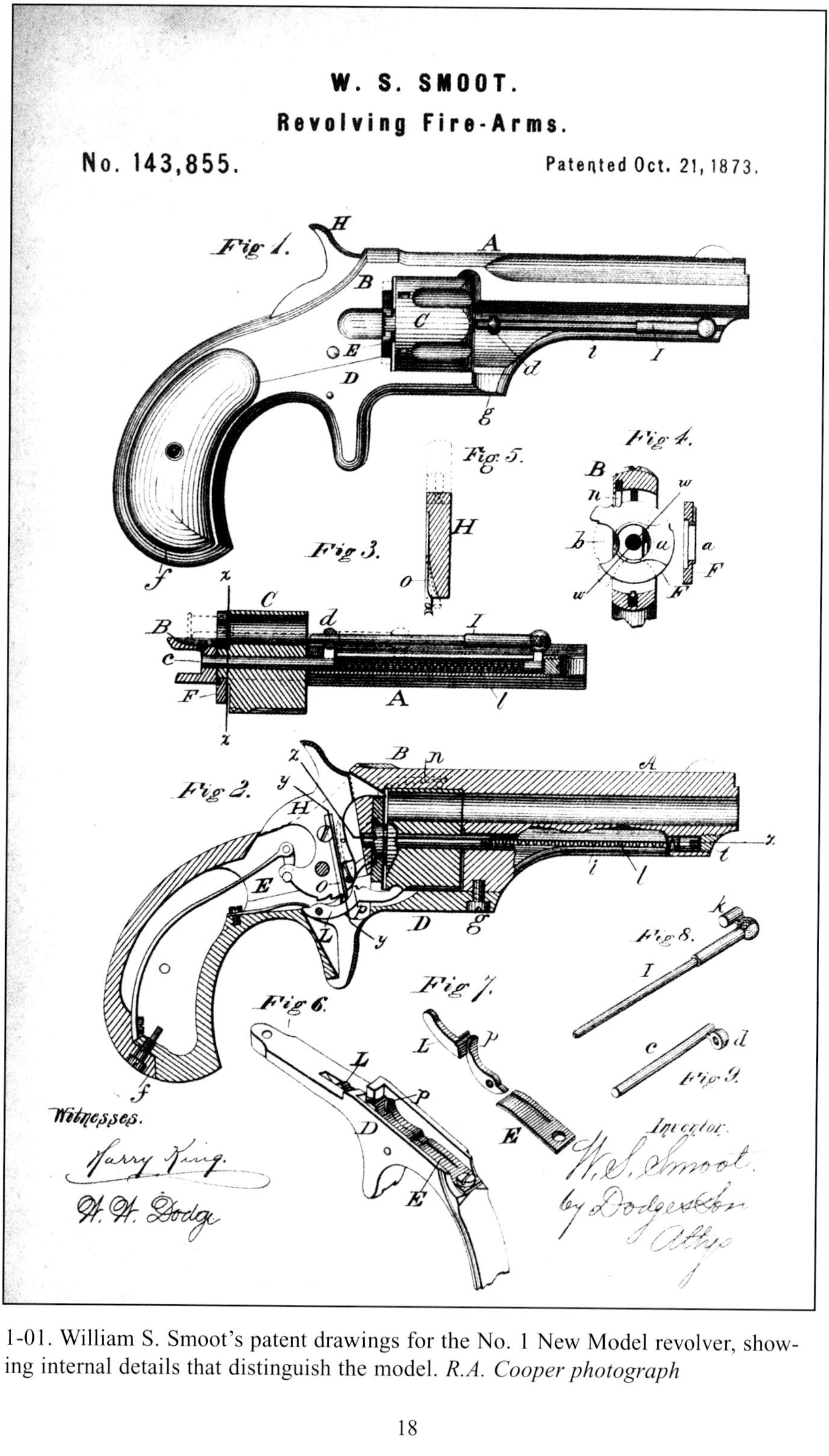

1-01. William S. Smoot's patent drawings for the No. 1 New Model revolver, showing internal details that distinguish the model. *R.A. Cooper photograph*

had experience similar to that of Remington with small-caliber pistols. For instance, Henry Deringer created a small percussion pocket pistol that gave his name to an entire class of pistols. For Remington, the result was the long-term production of its famous Double Derringer, a small arm that remained popular well into the twentieth century. The last one was produced in 1935.

While economic survival, competition, and the drive for innovation were obvious reasons for offering new and improved forms of revolvers and rifles, other forces were also present. Notable among the latter were international politics, and factors relating to military materiél improvements.

Still other factors affecting new handgun technology included America's westward expansion, its changing territorial demographics, and its postwar transition into the coming Industrial Age. Arms historian Harold Peterson[2] offered a view as to why Remington chose to expand into and emphasize small pistols. He felt Remington believed that less bulge in the pocket gained the advantage of an effective weapon with fewer shots. Whether a Double Derringer, or a small multi-shot pistol, the company believed their products would satisfy the wants of 1870s society.

These forces combined to initiate Remington's efforts to meet the needs of a modern market. In 1873 the same forces allowed William S. Smoot to obtain a patent for his new revolver design. In this chapter the authors have chosen to adopt the name of Smoot's firearm as used by Remington, including Remington's use of the grammatical possessive for Smoot. It will not be used hereafter. This was done with the knowledge that many readers will be unable to connect a familiar firearm image with the "No. 1" name. The cue, "Smoot's Patent," has caused the Smoot name to be applied erroneously to the Remington "No. 4" revolver, an error the senior author wrote about years earlier.[3] However, as late as 1980[4], and again in 1995[5], the error was still being perpetuated.

Smoot patent arms have frequently been referred to as "New Line," a label used by Karr and Karr[6], an early resource on Remington. However, Remington catalogs printed during the period referred to the revolver by the name used in this chapter. Agents and distributors apparently used the term "New Line," or another name of their choosing, in order to help sell the weapons. Examples of the foregoing include Lamberson, Furman & Company of New York, and the Lamberson Company of Chicago, sole agents for Remington arms from 1884 through 1887. In their catalogs these companies used "New Line" as a page heading, below which were illustrated engraved cuts of the No. 1 revolver and other Remington models.

W.S. Smoot was issued U.S. patent number 143,855, dated October 21, 1873, and titled "Improvement in Revolving Fire-Arms." While some have questioned why Remington was the assignee of one-half of any patent rights granted to employees of the firm, it was and still is common practice for anyone financed in an invention to assign some part of its value to the company. Considering Smoot's experience, combined with the Remington company's arms-making prestige, it follows that such a mutually attractive relationship would be validated in a shared patent.

Below the patent title, the first paragraph contains the essentials of the patent and marks it, as Smoot noted, an "improvement in revolvers." It states that, "My invention relates to that class of firearms known as revolvers; and the invention consists in a peculiar manner of forming the barrel and frame of a single piece of metal in connection with the guard strap; in a revolving recoil shield of novel construction; a novel construction and arrangement of the ejector and center pin, together with various other details of construction." Smoot used the adjective "novel" twice, perhaps appropriate for this period in firearms manufacture. Today we might call it "sound engineering" and "production efficiency." Only the revolving recoil shield (hereafter referred to as "RRS") feature with its complexity might conceivably be questioned for its role in the operation of the revolver (photo 1-01).

In defining the word "novel" as applied to Remington's No. 1 Smoot Patent revolver, one finds that the barrel and frame were milled from a solid forging, on a new milling machine designed by Smoot. The revolver's assembly and disassembly were relatively simple. The bottom of the frame presented access to the lock parts for cleaning and repair, while the housing for the ejector was milled out of the bottom of the barrel frame. The cylinder pin doubled as the rear guide for the ejector rod. A spring between the cylinder pin and ejector rod had two purposes. It provided tension to hold the ejector rod forward while concurrently keeping the cylinder in place to the rear. The cylinder pin featured an arched spring recessed in the shaft to control cylinder rotation. The entire assembly was fixed in place by a set-screw in the housing under the barrel muzzle. For the RRS, the loading gate/recoil shield was V-grooved and fit into a slot or groove milled into the top and bottom frame (photos 1-09, 1-10). The entire revolver, its disassembly, the small number of parts, its sturdy construction, symmetry of line, and general compact appearance all contributed much to Remington's reputation for fine firearms (photo 1-01).

Determining the period or date of production and sale of Remington products ideally would come from Remington catalogs or advertising price lists. However, a review of such documents reveals that Remington was inconsistent in producing those materials. Several presumed-yearly catalogs were printed with no publication dates or designation of edition. Advertising flyers also have been found without dates. Discussing one such company brochure, Landskron notes, "It is not dated, as many advertising items by the firm are found not to be."[7] Since the patent date of the No. 1 Smoot Patent revolver was October 1873, we would expect to find the model offered for sale in early 1874. Although copies of the 1874 catalog exist, it contains no announcement for the sale of the No. 1 revolver.

The first such announcement in an advertising price list was dated January 1875, and states the following:

New revolver—best in the world. Remington's No. 1 pocket revolver, new model using a .30 cartridge. Loaded and cartridge ejected without removing cylinder. Weight 10 oz., all steel, barrel and frame one solid piece. Price, full plate, $10.

No engraved cut or photograph was provided. A full-size Remington catalog, which was made available after February 1875, contained target shooting and reloading information as well as letters of testimonial from customers on their experiences with certain products. However, the 1875 price announcement was not repeated.

The above is an example of the value of corroborative records to establish the beginning date of sale for a particular arm. Remington's inconsistency and lack of dated annual publications handicap today's researchers. The company's practice of publishing undated advertising fliers, collateral to catalogs, also constrains the establishment of any accurate date of product sale. The January 1876 catalog featured a full-size engraving of the No. 1 Smoot Patent revolver along with basic information. It concluded with the statement that "all these revolvers are nickel-plated" (see Table 1-A). The 1877 catalog cited the availability of finishes in blue, full-plate, or nickeled, gilt, and engraved. It listed prices for ivory and pearl grips, but no mention was made of checkered hard-rubber "stocks," or grips. Even more was presented in the 1878 catalog, with information and availability of the No. 1, No. 2, No. 3 (bird-head grips, octagon barrel), and No. 4 revolvers. All four models were pictured, with caliber designations noted and prices for finishes as well as for ivory and pearl grips.

Remington No. 1 Revolver.

(Smoot's Patent,) New Model

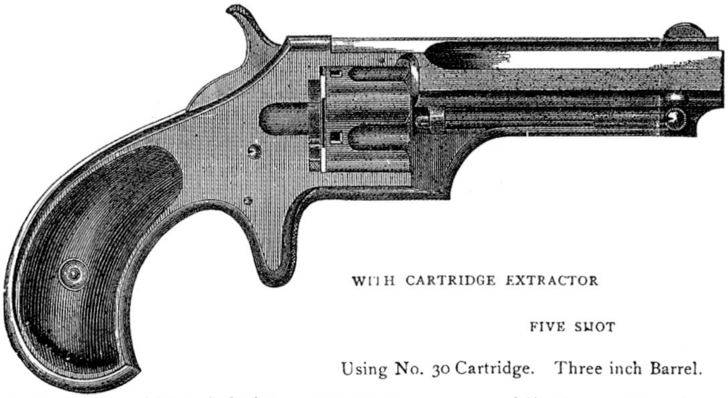

Length of Pistol 6¾ in. Weight 10 oz. All these Revolvers are finished in the BEST manner, with forged Steel Frames and Checkered Rubber Stocks.

For that period in Remington history, the senior author has concluded that Remington most likely perceived company publications as being ephemeral—here today, gone tomorrow. From 1874 to the receivership decision in 1886, there is no indication that Remington publications were meant to be enduring.

As for the question of how long the No. 1 revolver might have been advertised for sale, a review of the September 1, 1887 sole agent catalog (after receivership) finds the No. 1 pictured in "exact size," along with other models that will be noted in later chapters. Thus, approximately a decade of Remington-produced catalogs and price list flyers described the availability of the No. 1. Each year since 1875 bits of information were added, such as "checkered rubber stocks," and, of course, price increases.

Serial Number Data

Since the RRS feature appeared in the No. 1 revolver's patent description, it seems logical to expect extant revolvers to bear serial numbers that begin with the number "1." As a manufacturing change was made to the fixed recoil shield, one might hypothesize that no new numbering would need to take place. Since changes to the shield did not constitute a major modification, continuous numbering would have been logical and reasonable. Such was the case with the recording of data on all No. 1 revolvers observed and/or examined during the last four decades (see Tables 1-A and 1-B).

Descriptive data have been recorded for fifty-seven revolvers equipped with the RRS. The lowest recorded serial number is "1," and the highest is "667." The senior author has recorded the serial numbers for No. 1 specimens (see Tables 1-A and 1-B), all spaced by a range of 20 to 41 digits up to serial number "2976." Only one successive pair in the distribution differs by 102 digits.

Using intervals of 100, each indicated that fixed recoil shields were begun early in production. Presuming the serial numbering was sequential, this supports the view that a fixed shield was produced, or at least was available, as initial RRS specimens were being made. The RRS serial number intervals progress up to "700," and the fixed shield has eighteen serial numbered specimens in these same intervals. One can therefore infer that the fixed shield was produced, or least available, concurrently with the RRS. Table 1-C shows the RRS drop in production after serial number "400," since fewer specimens were recorded. RRS sampling for the first four intervals (44) represents 77% of the total number recorded. In the remaining intervals to serial number "700," less than half of the specimens were recorded compared to the first 400. This suggested that RRS production was limited, and that Remington made the decision early-on to produce the fixed shield.

Table 1-C portrays the fixed shield variation as essentially numbered after serial number "300," its incidence nearly as large (four intervals) as those for the RRS. The eighteen fixed shield specimens, serial numbered among the

Table 1-A

No. 1 revolving recoil shield and fixed shield sample frequency for all types of finish for all serial number intervals.

Serial Number Intervals	Revolving Recoil Shield				Fixed Shield			
	Nickel	Blue	Engraved	Total	Nickel	Blue	Engraved	Total
001 - 200	7	1	16	24			1	1
201 - 400	19		1	20	5			5
401 - 600	9			9	10			10
601 - 800	3		1	4	5		1	6
801 - 1000					11		1	12
1001 - 1200					6		1	7
1201 - 1400					7	1	4	12
1401 - 1600					9		4	13
1601 - 1800					3		7	10
1801 - 2000					6	2	8	16
2001 - 2200					4	5	1	10
2201 - 2400					2	1	1	4
2401 - 2600					7	1		8
2601 - 2800					12	2	1	15
2801 - 3000					4		2	6
TOTAL	38	1	18	57	91	12	32	135
Percentage	66.7%	1.7%	31.6%		64.8%	9.6%	25.6%	

*Not included in this table: Gold and mixed-finish specimens.

RRS specimens, represent approximately 32% of those observed. Table 1-C also reveals that for the RRS, beginning with serial number "301" all but one specimen was finished in nickel. For RRS specimens in the first three intervals, eighteen engraved pieces were recorded along with one in blue finish. Beginning with serial number "301" through seven intervals, only one RRS specimen has been recorded with engraved finish. This profile conveys the likelihood that, beginning with serial number "301," finishing any RRS revolvers in nickel con-

Table 1-B

No. 1 revolving recoil shield and fixed shield sample frequency for all types of grip materials for all serial number intervals.

Revolving Recoil Shield Grips

Serial # Intervals	1 Walnut	2 Rose.	3 Pearl	4 Cell.	5 Ivory	6 Chkr. Rubber	7 Sm. Rubber	8 Unknown
001 - 200	3	5	12		1	2		
201 - 400	9	8	2					1
401 - 600	3	5				2		
601 - 800		1	2			1		
801 - 1000								
TOTAL	15	19	16		1	5		1
Percentage	26.3%	33.3%	28.1%		1.7%	8.8%		1.7%

Fixed Shield Grips

Serial # Intervals	1 Walnut	2 Rose.	3 Pearl	4 Cell.	5 Ivory	6 Chkr. Rubber	7 Sm. Rubber	8 Unknown
001 - 200		1						
201 - 400	1	1	1			2		
401 - 600	1					9		
601 - 800		1	1	2		2		
801 - 1000	2		1	3	1	5		
1001 - 1200	1	1	2	0	0	3		
1201 - 1400	1	1	4	0	0	5		1
1401 - 1600	2		5	1	0	5		
1601 - 1800			3	4	1	2		
1801 - 2000	2	1	8	2	0	3		
2001 - 2200	1	2	1	4		2		
2201 - 2400	1		1			2		
2401 - 2600	1		1			5	1	
2601 - 2800	1	1	2			1		
2801 - 3000	1		1	2		2		
TOTAL	15	9	31	18	2	48	1	1
Percentage	12.0%	7.2%	24.8%	14.4%	1.6%	38.4	.8%	.8%

1. Walnut 2. Rosewood 3. Pearl 4. Celluloid 5. Ivory 6. Checkered Rubber 7. Smooth Rubber 8. Unknown

forms to what had occurred with the fixed shield, *i.e.*, only nickel-plated specimens were made.

It must be observed that the serial number break for the fixed recoil shield specimen is not definitive, although it is sufficiently indicative of transitional modification (see Table 1-C). Some interesting findings resulted when RRS serial number intervals were compared with fixed shield in the first seven intervals (see Table 1-C). In these seven intervals, RRS specimens exceed fixed shield by a factor of three. Looking at differences in finishes, RRS had 38 (66.7%) in nickel, and eighteen (31.6%) were engraved. The seventeen fixed shield specimens (94.4%) had nickel finish, and only one (5.5%) was engraved. Such differences in finish suggest that different production concepts were operative.

One possible explanation for the difference was that the fixed shield was quickly implemented to counter early complaints about the operation and repair of the RRS. Acquired facility in manufacturing the fixed shield would provide the public with a revolver that would counter the initial problems experienced with the RRS. Significant customer criticism about the RRS may have influenced early production of the fixed shield.

In the first seven intervals (see Table 1-C), the profile for finish and grip material portrayed the RRS and fixed shield specimens as two different revolvers. The fixed shield incidence, although initially tentative in serial number intervals, suggests that more sales effort was needed. It is reasonable to speculate that RRS production complexity, and repair criticism, probably combined to bring about the transition to the fixed shield early in the serial numbering.

No duplicate-numbered pieces were recorded, and no evidence has been found to suggest that Remington renumbered the No. 1, as was the case with other models. The senior author's research procedure and documentation of each piece are detailed enough to have encountered the same pieces at various gun collector shows throughout the past four decades.

Karr and Karr cited estimated production of over 20,000 for the No. 1 revolver[8], but with no published source of support. No documents have become available to either authenticate Remington production figures or to validate the Karr and Karr estimate. The authors' empiric data clearly contradicts the Karr and Karr production estimates. As further support for the authors' conclusions, no revolver has been recorded with a five-digit serial number. Of the more than 190 No. 1 revolvers represented in the sample, no duplicate-numbered revolvers were discovered. Had over 20,000 of these revolvers been produced, the probability of finding duplicate numbered revolvers in the sampling would have been significant. Since no systematic duplication exists, it may be concluded that only a small number were manufactured.

The matter of competition from other firearms manufacturers, the relative cost of the piece, the particular caliber, and the additional competition from other available models are regarded as factors influencing the total number actu-

Table 1-C

No. 1 revolving recoil shield and fixed shield sample frequency and comparison for finish and grip material in the first seven number intervals

Revolving Recoil Shield

	Finish			Grip Material							
Serial # Intervals	1 Nickel	2 Blue	3 Engr.	4 Wal.	5 Rose.	6 Pearl	7 Cell.	8 Ivory	9 Chkr. Rub.	10 Sm. Rub.	11 Unk.
001 - 100	2	1	9	1	1	9		1			
101 - 200	5		7	2	5	3			2		
201 - 300	9		1	4	3	2					1
301 - 400	10			5	5						
401 - 500	5			2	3						
501 - 600	4			1	1				2		
601 - 700	3		1		1	2			1		
TOTAL	38	1	18	15	19	16		1	5		1

Fixed Recoil Shield

	Finish			Grip Material							
Serial # Intervals	1 Nickel	2 Blue	3 Engr.	4 Wal.	5 Rose.	6 Pearl	7 Cell.	8 Ivory	9 Chkr. Rub.	10 Sm. Rub.	11 Unk.
001 - 100			1		1						
101 - 200											
201 - 300	1								1		
301 - 400	4			1	1	1			1		
401 - 500	4			1					3		
501 - 600	6								6		
601 - 700	2			1					1		
TOTAL	17		1	3	2	1			12		

1. Nickel 2. Blue 3. Engraved 4. Walnut 5. Rosewood 6. Pearl 7. Celluloid 8. Ivory 9. Checkered Rubber 10. Smooth Rubber 11. Unknown

*Not included in this table: Gold and mixed-finish specimens.

ally manufactured. The relatively short period of availability (1875 or 1876 to 1885) tends to further sustain the probability of limited production.

Estimates of No. 1 Production

The total number of No. 1 models was estimated, based on statistical techniques.[9] With fifty-seven observed specimens serial numbered from "1" to "667," it is estimated with a 95% confidence factor that as many as 703 could have been produced. For all No. 1 specimens, having both RRS and FS (192) observations, the estimate is that as many as 3,023 were manufactured.

Even though Remington catalogs and advertising price lists continued to show the No. 1 revolver's availability, this did not mean that manufacturing continued. The senior author believes that the No. 1 was initially made without finish and stored until an order came in. Finish and grips were then completed per the order. No record or statement has been found that indicates termination of production. When E. Remington & Sons went into receivership in 1886, it is quite likely that any incomplete No. 1 revolvers were finished for transfer to the company's sole sales agents.

Statistical Treatment

For each of the models, or its variations, the distribution of serial numbers was divided into intervals. No specimens were found in some of these intervals, even though with the number of specimens examined over the past forty years, it would be expected that, provided that Remington produced them, some would be found in each interval. That supposition was tested using a Chi-square goodness of fit analysis.[10] If the probability of the observed distribution was very small, say 1% or less, then the results would point to a non-chance distribution, one that indicates lack of production of models in certain serial number ranges.

For the No. 1 observations, and for each No. 2 caliber (.30 and .32), the observed distribution is significantly different from random, with only one chance in 1000 of concluding that there was no pattern to the distribution. This is also true of the No. 3 BHO (bird-head grip, octagon barrel) revolver, and all variants of the No. 4 model. The results for the No. 3 BHR (bird-head grip, ribbed barrel) are statistically significant at the chance level of two in 1000, which is still strongly convincing.

The other set of questions that can be answered statistically is the number produced of each model or its variant. By a complex statistical technique, illustrated in Noether[11], the lowest and highest serial number in a series along with the number of specimens observed were utilized to determine the probable number produced. The upper limit was determined based on a confidence factor selected to be 95%. The technique was modified by subtracting a constant for the models where the serial numbers began considerably higher than serial number "1", *i.e.*, the No. 3 BHR and SH (saw handle grip). Results of these computations are listed in the corresponding chapters.

Serial Number Location and Stamping Practice

Remington placed serial numbers on the left lower frame or under the left lower grip. For production facility, one set appears on the upper part of the frame and the other set on the lower. When the two frame sections are joined, the two sets of numbers appear side-by-side and are separated by the juncture (photo 1-02).

Several specimens exhibit an over-stamping of numbers. One specimen shows the over-stamp to have been a production error, since the correction involved a single digit. For each over-stamped specimen examined to date, the effort was clearly done with a Remington die rather than a later amateur attempt to alter the numbers.

Of further interest is the occasion of mixed-number revolvers. Several have been examined where the top portion of the frame has one set of digits, and the bottom part a different set. In these specimens, the manner in which both parts of the revolver were fitted, the finish, and the general condition point to the conclusion that the mixed numbering was most logically a factory error. One such specimen (serial number "1546/1646") examined is factory engraved and in fine condition, precluding the possibility of non-factory alteration.

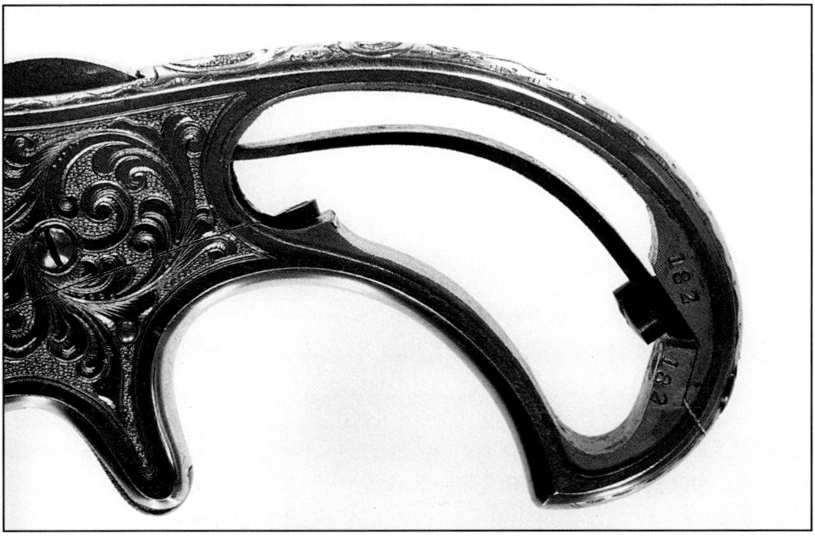

1-02. Detail view, showing serial number locations on left side of top and bottom frame halves. *R.A. Cooper photograph*

The matter of a discrepancy of one digit in the two sets of serial numbers has been observed. One such revolver bears serial numbers "1941" and "1942," and was factory engraved. Since the condition is fine or better, the two sets of numbers must be regarded as a production stamping error. In these cases the numbers are quite clear and obviously not over-stamped. No specimen of the No. 1 revolver is known or has been examined that has factory serial numbers elsewhere on the frame.

Identifying Features of the Model No. 1

Caliber Data

E. Remington & Sons catalogs of the period (1877-1883) consistently state that the No. 1 model was offered in .30 caliber rimfire short. No Remington-produced specimen has been examined or is known to be of smaller, or larger, caliber. It is conceivable that an individual might have special ordered a caliber, *e.g.*, .22, that was within the engineering capability of the model. The question arises regarding Remington's response to fulfilling a requested barrel, caliber, or other machining variation, as well as finish. Karr and Karr state, "It would be well to reiterate that Remington did custom gunsmithing. Whatever a customer wanted, within the bounds of reason, he could have. It is entirely possible that a collector will turn up a gun with almost any sort of variation from standard models."[12] A blunt counterpoint to this view was revealed in a letter Remington addressed to a customer in August 1871. It stated, "Replying to yours of August 19th, I would say we manufacture no guns except such as described in the enclosed list, all of regular pattern and breech loading."[13] A fairly terse business communication, this note seems to discourage deviation from standard production line work.

More supportive of Remington's position is the lack of existing recorded specimens that underwent obvious changes to the standard No. 1 model. Finish and engraving detail were generally reasonable requests which, from experience, Remington was able to handle economically. Changes in caliber, especially beyond the safety restraints, were readily denied a customer. Physical change to revolver dimensions would most likely have been rejected, as well. It is of interest to note that the No. 1, being rather small, was never offered in .22 caliber, although the caliber was available from Remington in its "Vest Pocket" model. Other companies of this period manufactured small .22 caliber pistols, so this caliber was reasonably popular. The likelihood of securing a caliber larger than .30 is doubtful from a technical viewpoint. In short, no factory-produced specimen has been examined nor is known to exist having a caliber smaller or larger than the specified .30. It appears that the No. 1 revolver in .30 caliber was nonetheless popular, when compared to the production figures of the No. 2 revolver in .32 caliber.

Some speculation is possible on the popularity of the .30 caliber, as it relates to the probable number of guns produced. Certainly this caliber did not compete with either the .32 or .38, both of which were regular lines in nearly all firearms companies. Accuracy, hitting power, and cartridge availability in the marketplace were all important buyer considerations. When the No. 1 was compared with the Nos. 2, 3, and 4, recorded data clearly show a small number of specimens extant when the criterion was availability/survivability. Further, modern availability, principally at gun shows, finds the No. 1 significantly limited compared to the presence of other models. One might therefore infer that limited production existed. It is important to note that the patent description did not indicate caliber designation, but that data on 192 revolvers reveals that .30 caliber was the factory-produced bore. This is supported by both catalog descriptions and sales advertising.

Finishes

Catalogs from the period indicate the No. 1 revolver was available in "full plate," meaning nickel plate. Blued, engraved, and specially plated finishes were also available, but nickel plate was clearly the popular finish of the day. The sample indicates that 68.4% of the RRSs were nickel plated. Engraved specimens involved 29.8%. A sampling of specimens having a fixed recoil shield reveals 64% observed in nickel plate. Only one RRS specimen has been recorded with a blue finish. In the fixed recoil shield, twelve specimens (9.6%) of the sample have blue finish, while twelve (26.4%) were engraved (see Table 1-A).

Engraved specimens were common to all the production models offered by Remington (photo 1-03). Remington factory engraving appears to have a distinctive pattern, or identity, and therefore is discernable from any other company's engraving style. The distinctive swirls and floral-like lacing suggest a style apparently created by a single engraver, or possibly several engravers who followed a prescribed pattern. Gilt (or gold) finish was offered, with the buyer apparently specifying which revolver components were to be so treated. Recorded specimens with the RRS display a mixed finish, usually gold, on cylinder or hammer (see page 43). Specimens with a fixed recoil shield have been noted having gold on the hammer, cylinder, and ejector rod (see page 44). This includes specimens with all surfaces finished in gold.

Curiously, the Remington catalogs from 1877 to 1883 do not describe the two kinds of gold finish available. All specimens seen of the No. 1 revolver have had gold wash, a thinner, duller finish easily distinguished from gold plating, which results in a more reflective finish. No specimen entirely finished in gold plating has been examined, but this was assumed to have been available, as other Remington models finished in such a manner have been examined.

Specimens having a mixed finish provide contrast with the remaining nickel or other plated surfaces. It should be noted also that one specimen was

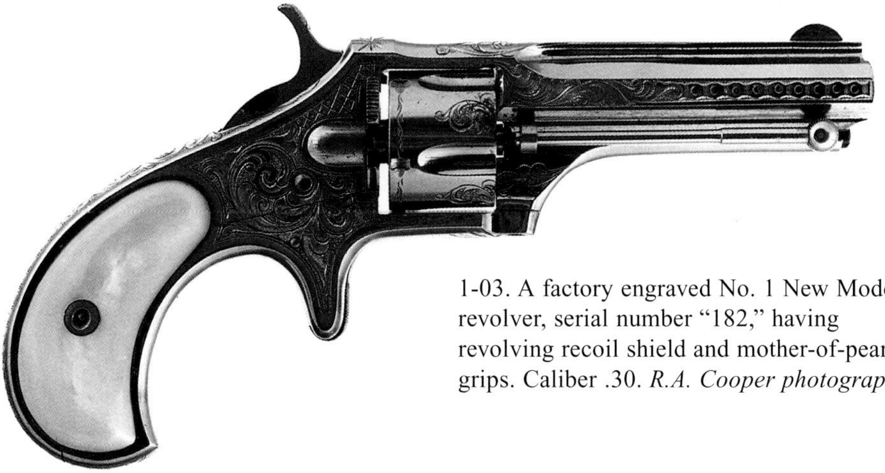

1-03. A factory engraved No. 1 New Model revolver, serial number "182," having revolving recoil shield and mother-of-pearl grips. Caliber .30. *R.A. Cooper photograph*

examined that was engraved and had a blued hammer (serial number "75"). It may be assumed that silver plate could have been ordered for the finish of a piece, even though it was not specifically indicated in the catalog. This may have been interpreted under the designation "plated" found in the catalog, as some specimens were recorded which were finished in that manner.

With respect to engraving, there seems to have been no "grading," or levels of engraved products available to the buyer. The catalogs make no statement regarding engraving coverage, nor was the buyer offered any sketch of how a factory engraved piece would appear. Engraving was done on easily seen surfaces, usually on both sides of the barrel (excluding the top rib) and on the backstrap. Generally no engraving appeared on the trigger. Cylinders were engraved in a large swirl design, with each flute constituting a separation. Flutes were left in plain finish corresponding to the rest of the piece. No specimen has been recorded with engraving in the flutes (photo 1-03).

Types of Grips

Recorded specimens possess grips reflecting the range of materials offered by Remington. Curiously, for the No. 1 revolver the 1877 catalog did not expressly offer the buyer walnut grips; rather, only ivory and pearl were the advertised grip materials. As both walnut and rosewood grips have been found on specimens, their omission in the catalog suggests that jobbers or retailers requested a specific type of wood. Table 1-B portrays both the RRS and fixed shield grip materials. Of the 57 RRS specimens, 34 (59.6%) had wood grips, five (9%) had grips of checkered hard rubber, and 16 (28%) had pearl grips. For the 135 fixed shield specimens, wood was found on 24 (19.2%), checkered hard rubber on 48 (38.4%), and pearl recorded on 31 (24.8%). Eighteen (14.4%) Remington celluloid gripped specimens were recorded, along with two (1.6%) which had genuine ivory, one

(.8%) with smooth rubber, and one (.8%) having an unknown material. Remington catalogs of the 1870s period did not inform the customer that checkered rubber grips were typically fitted on a basic nickel plated or blued revolver. The 1881 catalog marked the first time that "rubber stocks" were noted.

On most of the engraved specimens recorded, pearl grips seemed to complement the quality of work. It was the most expensive grip material, as identified in Remington catalogs for at least a decade. Personal communications with author Karl F. Moldenhauer[14] revealed some evidence that Remington may have experimented with imitation pearl. The grips on serial number "644" in his collection appeared more translucent and mottled than genuine pearl.[15] Several engraved pieces were known to have checkered rubber and Remington celluloid grips, but it was not discerned if the grips were ordered with these particular specimens.

Many antique arms dealers and collectors have erroneously described the ivory-colored celluloid grips used by Remington as "ivory." The senior author believed very early that these grips were of some hard rubber composition. Acceptance of "fact" from other individuals without documentation caused the senior author to pursue tests to support writings. A July 4, 1974 consultation with I.C. Stone, Ph.D., forensic chemist at the Institute of Forensic Science in Dallas, provided the following analysis, originally reported in the December 1974 issue of *Arms Gazette*: "A portion of the grips was analyzed by chemical and infrared spectrophotometric techniques. It is easily identifiable as nitrocellulose." Dr. Stone cited the text *Handbook of Common Polymers*[16], which observed that cellulose nitrate was plasticized in the U.S. by J.W. Hyatt in 1869. Hyatt manufactured and sold his product as "artificial ivory," which in turn led to its employment for other purposes, including dental plates under the name "celluloid" in 1871. This may be said to be the debut of the earliest form of plastic material.

The senior author's collection has several specimens of all models with celluloid grips. When compared with genuine ivory, some similarity is seen. However, the age lines and color shading common to old ivory are not the same in the celluloid grips. In terms of wear and appearance, the celluloid grips were adequate. However, chipping and cracking were common, resembling the characteristics of hard rubber. None of the RRS sample specimens recorded possess celluloid grips, although with the fixed recoil shield, eighteen (14.4%) of the recorded specimens had this grip material. One specimen examined in the RRS sample had genuine ivory grips, as do two fixed shield pieces. Most of the celluloid grips were molded over a steel backing, or plate, to provide support (photo 1-04). Since other models with these same grips exist, it seems probable that Remington had a "celluloid" molding machine set up to produce grips.

It is also significant that the Remington 1877 catalog and those that followed in 1883 did not distinguish in any manner the ivory-color celluloid described above. The catalogs merely indicated "ivory" and "pearl" grips, with

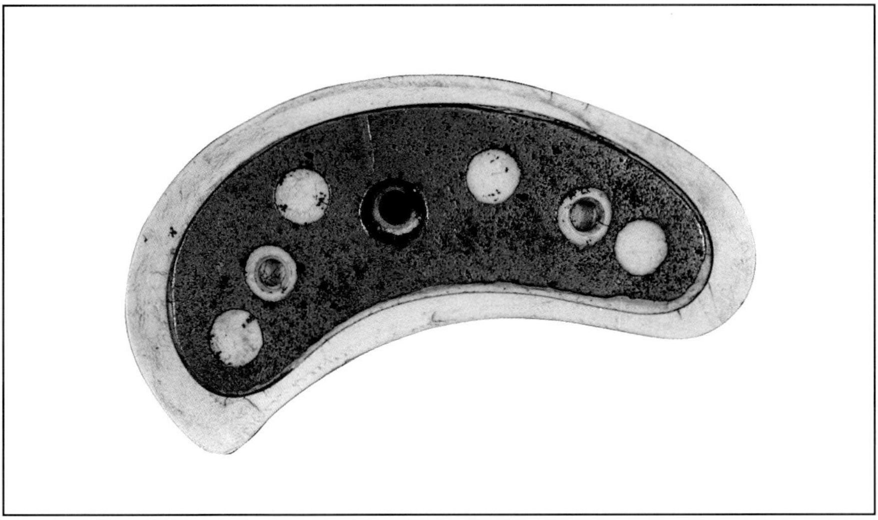

1-04. Detail view showing the steel backing plate used to reinforce the "imitation ivory" or molded celluloid grip. *R.A. Cooper photograph*

no explanatory comments offered. It seems misleading, even fraudulent, that Remington would offer a grip material readily mistaken for ivory without some explanation to the contrary in its sales literature. As further lack of clarification, the 1877 catalog and those that followed did not indicate checkered hard rubber as a grip alternative. Strangely, the engraving cut of the No. 1 revolver in the 1877 catalog shows what was meant to simulate wood as the grip material. None of the engraving cuts show checkering to portray hard rubber grips.

Hammer

On all No. 1 revolvers the hammer was case-hardened, in view of its wear and purpose. The firing pin was located in the nose of the hammer, and virtually none have been noted showing any damage. Essentially, the pin was flat-sided, with no specimen found that had a conical firing pin (photo 1-01). Generally, case-hardening with its colors offered a pleasant contrast to the nickel plating on a piece. Most specimens had their hammer case-hardened rather than in the finish of the revolver. All hammers had knurling or milling striations cut into the spur. Presumably this was to aid in finger control when retracting or releasing the hammer during use. The RRS specimens had milling done diagonally across the spur, while fixed recoil shield specimens had knurling or striations perpendicular to the sides of the hammer and spur, which give a more checkered effect (photos 1-05 and 1-06).

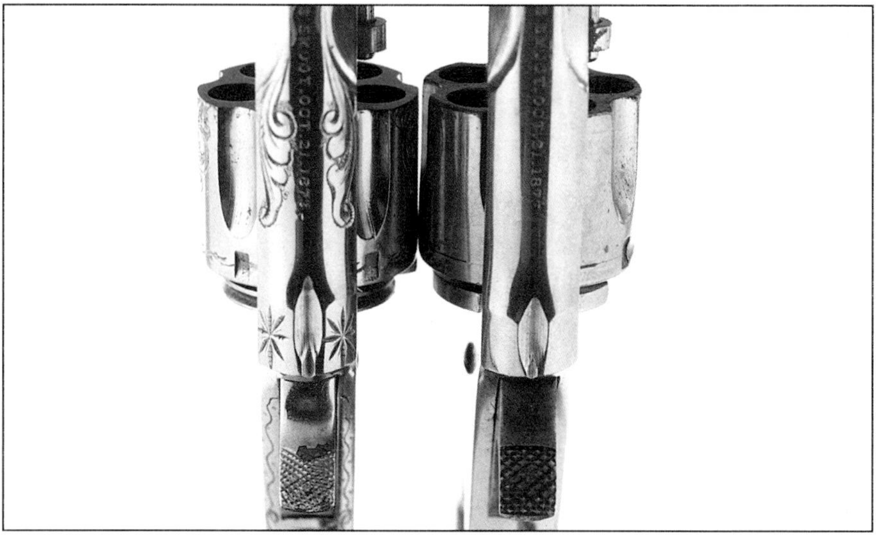

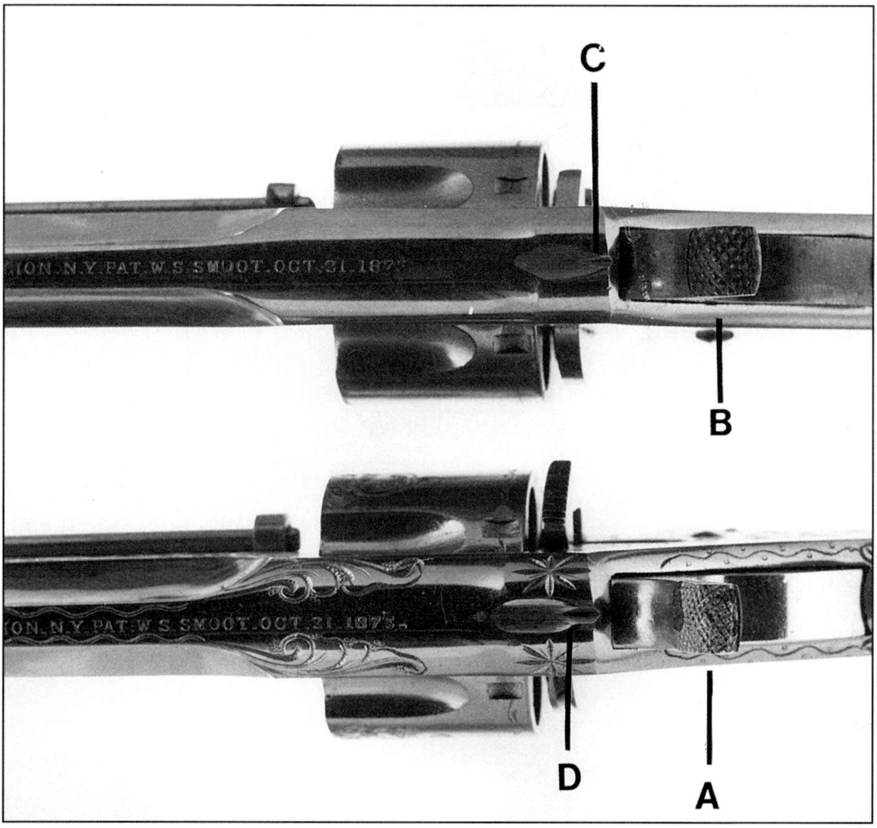

C
ION. N.Y. PAT. W.S. SMOOT. OCT. 21. 1873
B
ON. N.Y. PAT. W.S. SMOOT. OCT. 21. 1873.
D
A

1-05. (Opposite page, top). Detail view of top surfaces of two No. 1 New Model revolvers. Revolving recoil shield (left), fixed recoil shield (right). Note difference in cross-hatch patterns on hammer spurs. *R.A. Cooper photograph*

Trigger

On No. 1 revolvers the trigger is generally blued, although some case-hardened specimens have been recorded. Several revolvers have been noted with the trigger finished like the entire arm. The trigger face was produced with milled diagonal striations or knurling (photo 1-07). Since the No. 1 revolver had no triggerguard, it is assumed the trigger striations, like those on the hammer spur, were to insure firm finger contact. The lack of depth in this milling feature, along with the short, stubby trigger and frame housing, raises questions about the effectiveness of both. It is interesting to note that the No. 3 and No. 4 models have trigger faces with smooth surfaces.

Springs

All metal used for internal springs was tempered, and of good quality. Of the various springs in the No. 1 revolver, only the ejector rod spring has proved less than durable. In this spring, it would appear that the gauge or temper of the metal affected the maintenance of its original shape. Collapse and breakage were noted on many specimens. All springs were blued to deter corrosion, and none have been examined that were treated in any other manner.

The mainspring serving the hammer had unique features which proved reliable. No specimen examined showed any fault with its design. Photo 1-09 shows this feature, especially the T-fitting on the spring and the location on the hammer with its claw used to secure it. While the mainspring was secured to the grip fame with a screw, there appears to be no provision for any variation of tension on the spring by the screw that secures it (photo (1-02).

Screws

All screws on the No. 1 revolver were soft, and easily misshaped by the use of improperly sized screwdrivers. All screws were blued, although several specimens have been examined on which gold washed and/or nickel plated screws were employed.

1-06. (Opposite page, bottom). Detail view of top surfaces of two No. 1 New Model revolvers. Revolving recoil shield at bottom, with fine knurling on hammer spur (A) and large rear sight groove (D). Fixed recoil shield at top, with coarse knurling on hammer spur (B) and small rear sight groove (C). *R.A. Cooper photograph*

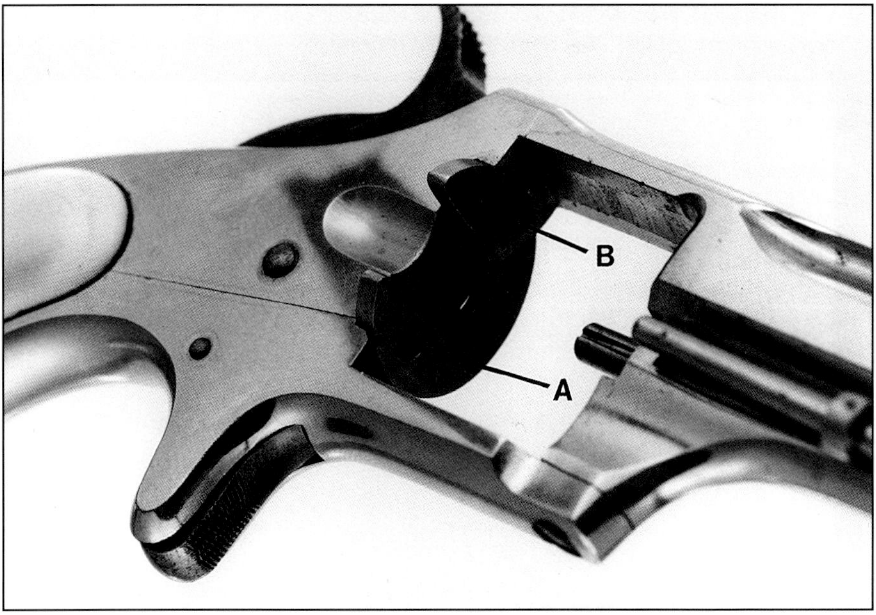

1-07. Detail view of right side of a No. 1 New Model revolver, showing fixed recoil shield with single retaining screw (A) and raised surface on forward portion of the shield (B) which prevents oversize cartridges from lining up in firing position.
R.A. Cooper photograph

Markings

All No. 1 revolvers were marked on the barrel with "E. Remington & Sons, Ilion, N.Y., Pat. W.S. Smoot, Oct. 21, 1873" in one line, reading from muzzle to hammer. It was the primary marking identifying a revolver, and no variation in type font has been noted. Also, no variation has been noted in the company title.

Some RRS specimens had either a number or a symbol stamped, usually on the rear face of the cylinder. The cylinder was not uniformly marked. On some specimens etched circles have been seen surrounding each chamber on the front of the cylinder. Their significance has not been determined. No chamber circles appear on specimens with fixed recoil shield. Several specimens with fixed recoil shield have been noted having digits on the cylinder, but they are unrelated to the serial number of the piece. Instead, they appear to be an assembly number used in the Remington production process. The No. 1 revolver has no uniform marking of its component parts.

Sights

Front sights on all No. 1 models were of uniform size ($^{13}/_{32}$ inch wide by $^{1}/_{8}$

inch high), nickel plated, and recessed into the barrel rib $^{1}/_{8}$ inch behind the muzzle. The rear sight was an oval-like notch milled into the top of the frame (photo 1-06). No specimen examined has any other type of factory-produced sight variation.

Barrel and Frame Assembly

The No. 1 revolver had a uniform $2^{3}/_{16}$ inch long barrel of basically octagonal shape, with a circular channel web below, and a top rib extending the entire length of the barrel. The barrel, the top rib, and the circular channel web were machined from a single piece of steel (photo 1-10). The circular channel web beneath the barrel houses the cylinder center pin, ejector spring, ejector pin lug, and ejector channel screw. The top rib is of uniform size ($^{5}/_{32}$ inch high by $^{1}/_{8}$ inch wide), and no variations have been noted. All barrels have five-groove rifling. Clearly, the machining and milling processes were multiple and complex, subject to possible errors, and probably resulted in considerable production scrap. The bottom portion of the revolver had less machining and is clearly smaller in size than the top portion. Essentially, the bottom frame houses the trigger and trigger spring (photo 1-08). One wonders what prompted Remington to produce a "low-price" revolver with such complex, multiple milling operations. Certainly the barrel and frame assembly is sturdy and cannot be faulted as unsafe in either design or operation.

Cylinder Center Pin and Shell Ejection System

A unique patent feature of the No. 1 revolver is its cylinder center pin and shell ejection system, which are part of the milling design of the barrel. Photos 1-01 and 1-07 show the manner in which each part relates to this overall function. The cylinder center pin ($1^{3}/_{8}$ inches long by $^{1}/_{8}$ inch wide) is made of high-quality steel with a washer-like lug machined onto its end. The center pin lug was designed to hold the ejector rod, as it had a hole bored into it equal to the circumference of the smaller dimension of the ejector rod. The cylinder center pin has a spring recessed into the shaft in an arched position to control revolutions, and to keep it from sliding out of the cylinder. This spring is reasonably sturdy, although the ease of firing is affected when the spring is bent or damaged. Any change in the angle of the cylinder center pin—due to a flattened spring or misalignment of the lug—affects not only the performance of the cylinder, but of the entire weapon. Also, any change in the center pin angle affects its ease of removal from the channel web tube.

The ejector rod was designed to have a lateral projection of cylindrical/circular shape made to slide along the tube-like web beneath the barrel. The ejector rod itself was made up of two circumferences, referred to by Somers as "two-stepped."[17] The smaller circumference is 1½ inches long, and the rod is $2^{3}/_{8}$ inches overall (photos 1-01 and 1-10). The smaller circumference was designed to allow travel beyond the back of the cylinder. The remaining larger

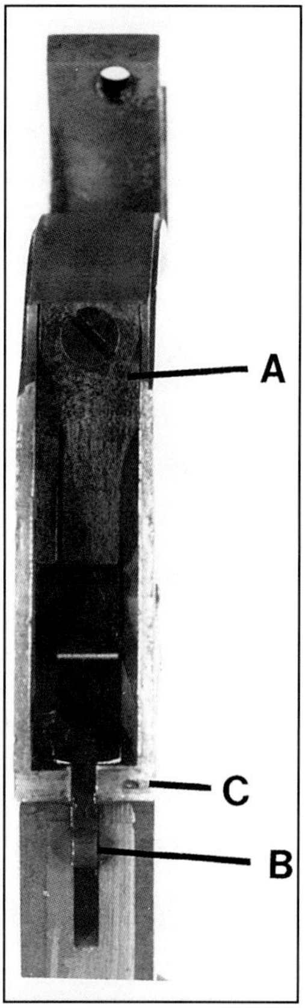

1-08. Detail view of bottom portion of frame of a No. 1 New Model revolver, showing trigger spring and screw (A), cylinder stop (B), and revolving recoil shield guide (C). *R.A. Cooper photograph*

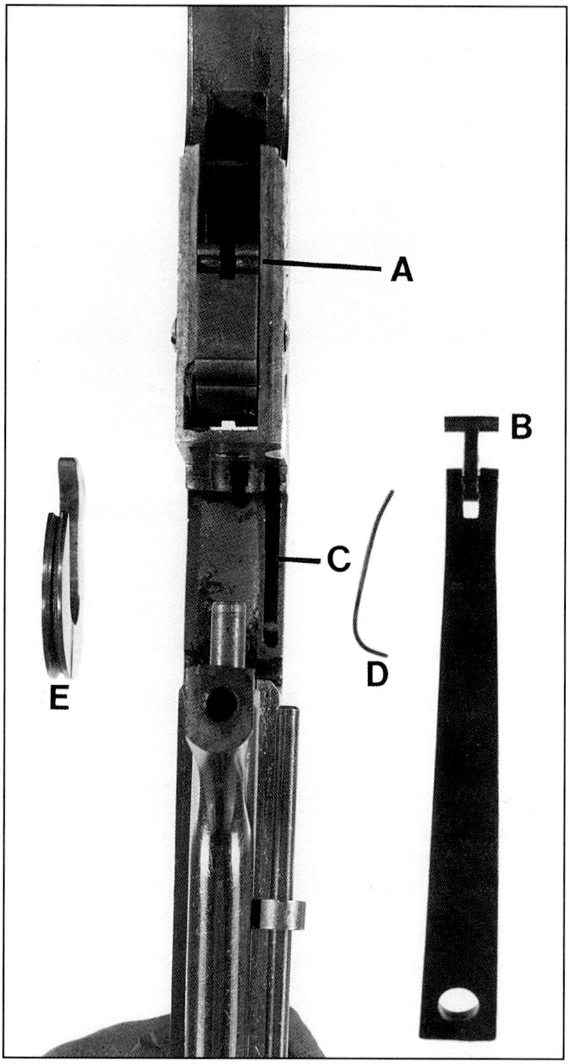

1-09. Detail view of top portion of frame of a No. 1 New Model revolver, showing hammer cut-out (A) that engages pivoting T-arm on mainspring (B), recoil shield spring recess (C), recoil shield spring (D) that engages recoil shield (E) with V-groove along outer edge. *R.A. Cooper photograph*

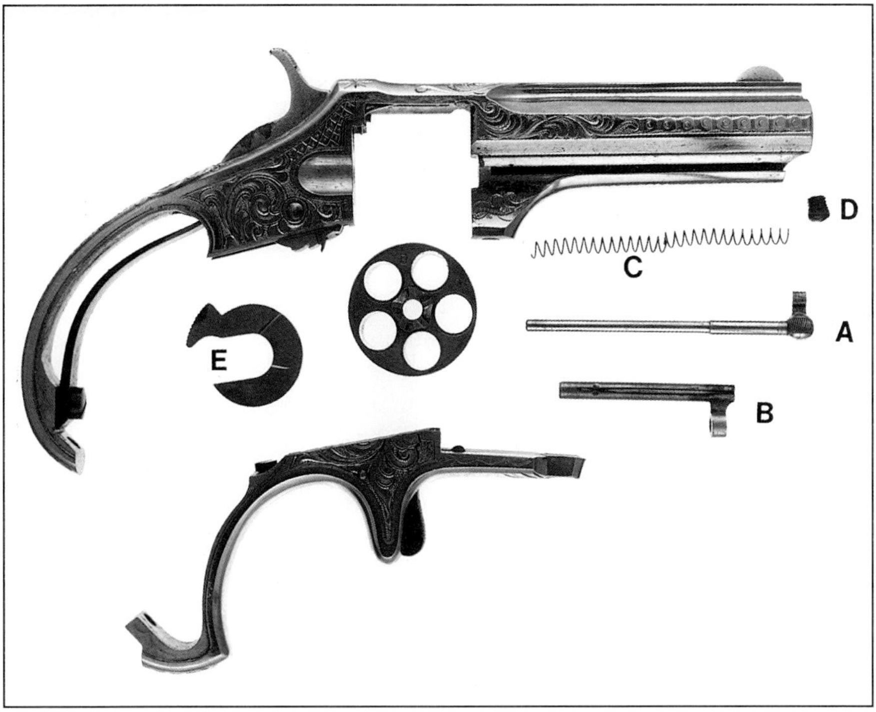

1-10. Disassembled view of a No. 1 New Model revolver, showing component parts: upper and lower frame halves, cylinder, ejector rod (A), cylinder pin (B), ejector spring (C), ejector channel screw (D), revolving recoil shield (E). *R.A. Cooper photograph*

circumference of the ejector rod eliminates the possibility of damaging the spring by compressing it too tightly. That clearly would affect the performance of the revolver, specifically by preventing the ejector rod from moving freely or from sliding into the chambers. The ejector spring should be in an extended position in order to provide enough tension to keep the ejector rod at the muzzle end. The tension on the ejector rod lug keeps it at its maximum extension. Removing the screw below the muzzle makes all elements in the tube-like channel accessible for cleaning or repair. It should be noted that in the later No. 2 revolver, this screw was replaced by a pin inserted perpendicular to the channel (photo 1-10).

While the two-step ejector rod is a distinguishing element of the RRS, fixed shield specimens were also equipped with the same style ejector rod. The Moldenhauer Collection featured a notable example: a No. 1 specimen with a single circumference ejector rod.[18] Such a rod became standard on the No. 2 revolver.

As noted earlier, the ejector rod and spring proved to be the weakest elements in the No. 1 revolver's design. While intended to keep tension on the ejector rod when not in use, any reduction in size and length of the spring affects the shell ejection operation. Many specimens have been examined with damaged cylinder pins, bent lugs, bent ejector rods, and dented channel web slots. The cylinder center pin and shell ejector system are, nevertheless, effective, and novel design features of this revolver.

Bushings

The patent drawing for the No. 1 revolver showed no detail for a bushing on the front of the cylinder, nor any cutout in the frame to accommodate such a bushing (photo 1-01). The size of the bushing and the minimal frequency of the bushing notch in the frame for RRS specimens (photos 1-03 and 1-11) suggest that production experience provided the basis for changes leading to the fixed shield on No. 1 RRS specimens. Serial numbers "452" and "644," pictured in the catalog of the Moldenhauer Collection[19], are other examples that display the notch in the frame for the cylinder bushing. Even though the patent drawing was for the RRS, a review of all recorded specimens indicates only 23% had a bushing on the cylinder (photo 1-03, and Table 1-D). Analysis of the serial numbers indicates no concentration within the intervals. Bushings for the RRS and fixed recoil shield vary in dimension from $^{1}/_{16}$ inch to $^{3}/_{32}$ inch. No records are available regarding the rationale for the procedures and incorporation into the fixed shield model No. 1. A ratchet bushing ($^{5}/_{32}$ inch) on the back of the cylinder is uniform on all No. 1 revolvers, having five claws to engage a pawl connected to the hammer. This serves to rotate the cylinder.

Cylinders

The cylinder is generally uniform for the five-shot revolver, although cylinders vary from .750 inch to .812 inch long. All have five flutes $^{9}/_{16}$ inch long by ¼ inch wide. Cylinder stop notches are uniform, and no variations in milling have been seen regarding any aspects of the cylinder.

Milling

A few milling variations were noted, particularly in the change from RRS to fixed recoil shield. Initial examination of RRS specimens revealed that some possessed etched-like or stamped circles around the front of each chamber. Over time this detail was recorded for thirty-one (54.4%) specimens (see Table 1-D). On some pieces the circles appear as a product or result of the process used for boring cylinder chambers. Other RRS examples examined suggest some design attribute. However, to the viewer no discernible purpose can be identified for the circles, as they do not have engraved quality.

On the RRS there is a beveling off of the frame where it meets the front

text continues on page 49

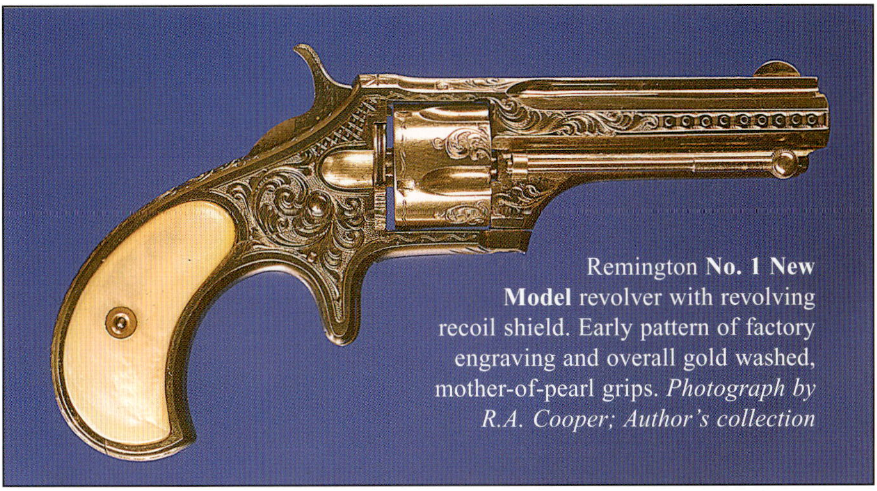

Remington **No. 1 New Model** revolver with revolving recoil shield. Early pattern of factory engraving and overall gold washed, mother-of-pearl grips. *Photograph by R.A. Cooper; Author's collection*

Remington **No. 1 New Model** revolver with fixed recoil shield, serial number "1881." Factory engraved and nickel plated with gold washed cylinder and hammer, mother-of-pearl grips. Factory wooden casing. *Photograph courtesy Paul Goodwin from* The Guns of Remington; *F. "Slim" Kohler collection*

Remington **No. 1 New Model** revolver with fixed recoil shield, serial number "1317." Factory engraved and silver plated with gold washed cylinder, celluloid "ivory" grips. Pipe-style casing. *Photograph courtesy Paul Goodwin from* The Guns of Remington; *Gordon Stanley collection*

Remington **No. 1 New Model** revolver with revolving recoil shield, serial number "9." Factory engraved and nickel plated, mother-of-pearl grips. Factory wooden casing. *Photograph courtesy Paul Goodwin from* The Guns of Remington; *Robert J. Allen collection*

Remington **No. 1 New Model** revolver with revolving recoil shield, serial number "206." Factory engraved and silver plated with gold washed cylinder, monogrammed mother-of-pearl grips. Pipe-style casing. *Photograph courtesy Paul Goodwin from* The Guns of Remington; *L. Richard Littlefield collection*

Remington **No. 1 New Model** revolver with fixed recoil shield, serial number "1511." Factory engraved and nickel plated with gold washed cylinder and hammer, mother-of-pearl grips. *Photograph courtesy Paul Goodwin from* The Guns of Remington; *Richard J. Shepler collection*

Remington **No. 1 New Model** revolver with fixed recoil shield, serial number "2036." Factory engraved and silver plated with gold washed cylinder and hammer, mother-of-pearl grips. *Photograph courtesy Paul Goodwin from* The Guns of Remington; *L. Richard Littlefield collection*

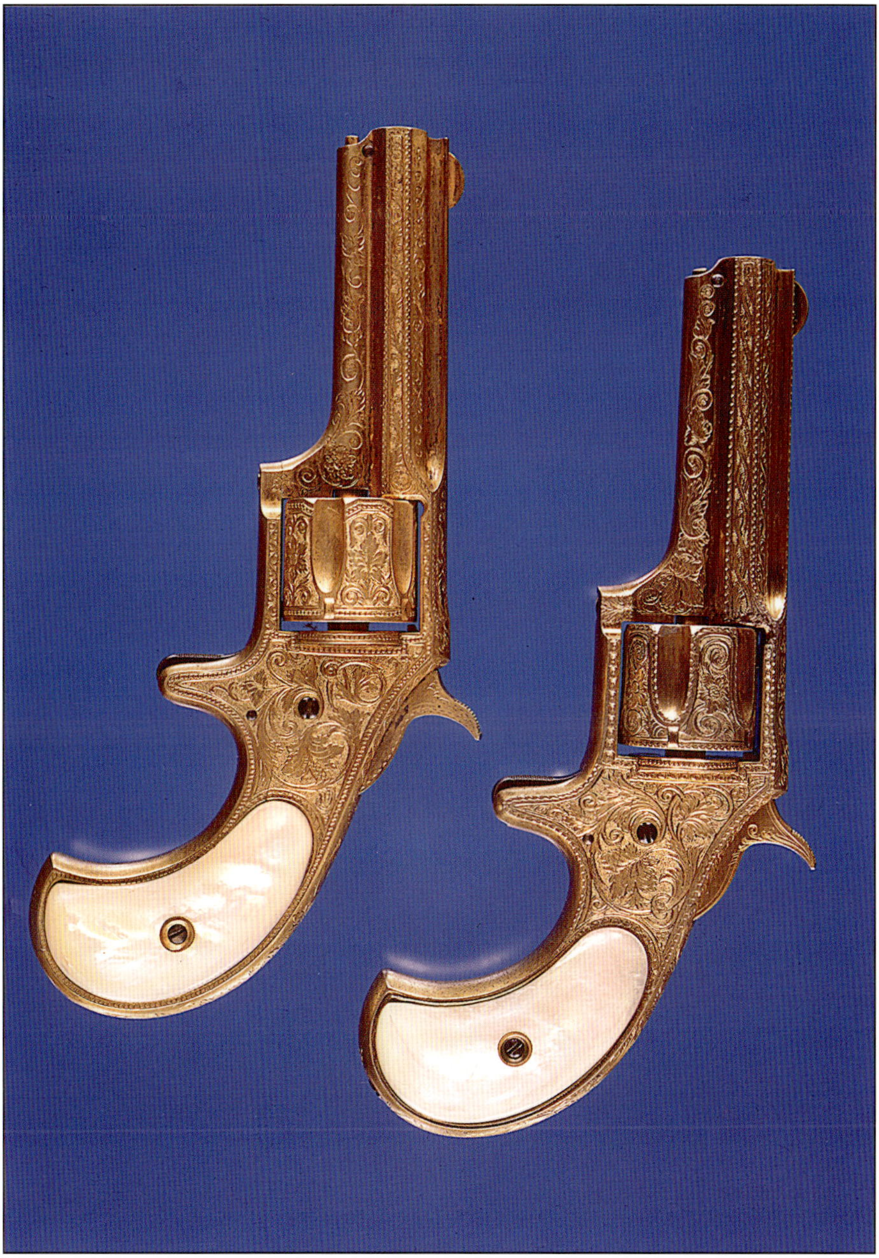

A pair of nearly-identical Remington **No. 2 New Model** Smoot's Patent revolvers. The factory engraving on each is unusually ornate, well beyond that which is factory standard. These pistols are overall gold washed, and fitted with genuine mother-of-pearl grips. Caliber .32. The serial numbers are "871" (left) and "977" (right). *Photograph by R.A. Cooper; Private collections*

Remington **No. 3 New Model** revolver with bird-head grip, serial number "13696." Factory engraved and nickel plated, celluloid "ivory" grips, octagonal barrel with large front sight. Caliber .38 rimfire. *Photograph courtesy Paul Goodwin from* The Guns of Remington; *F. "Slim" Kohler collection*

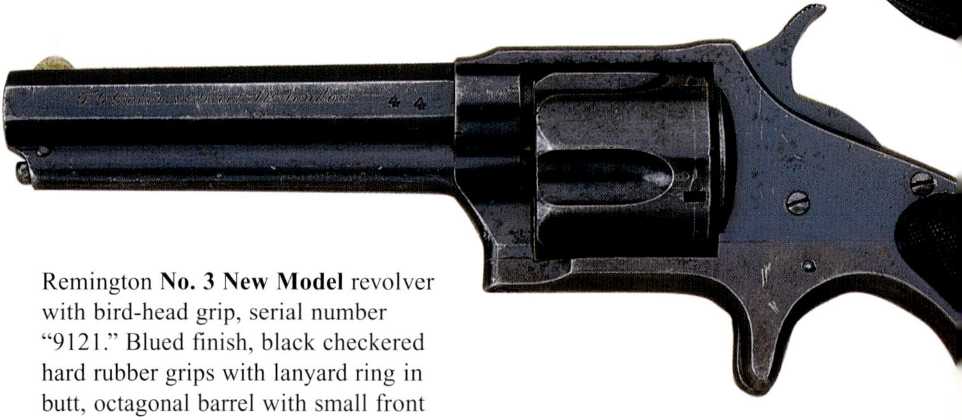

Remington **No. 3 New Model** revolver with bird-head grip, serial number "9121." Blued finish, black checkered hard rubber grips with lanyard ring in butt, octagonal barrel with small front sight. Caliber .38 centerfire. *Photograph courtesy Paul Goodwin from* The Guns of Remington; *F. "Slim" Kohler collection*

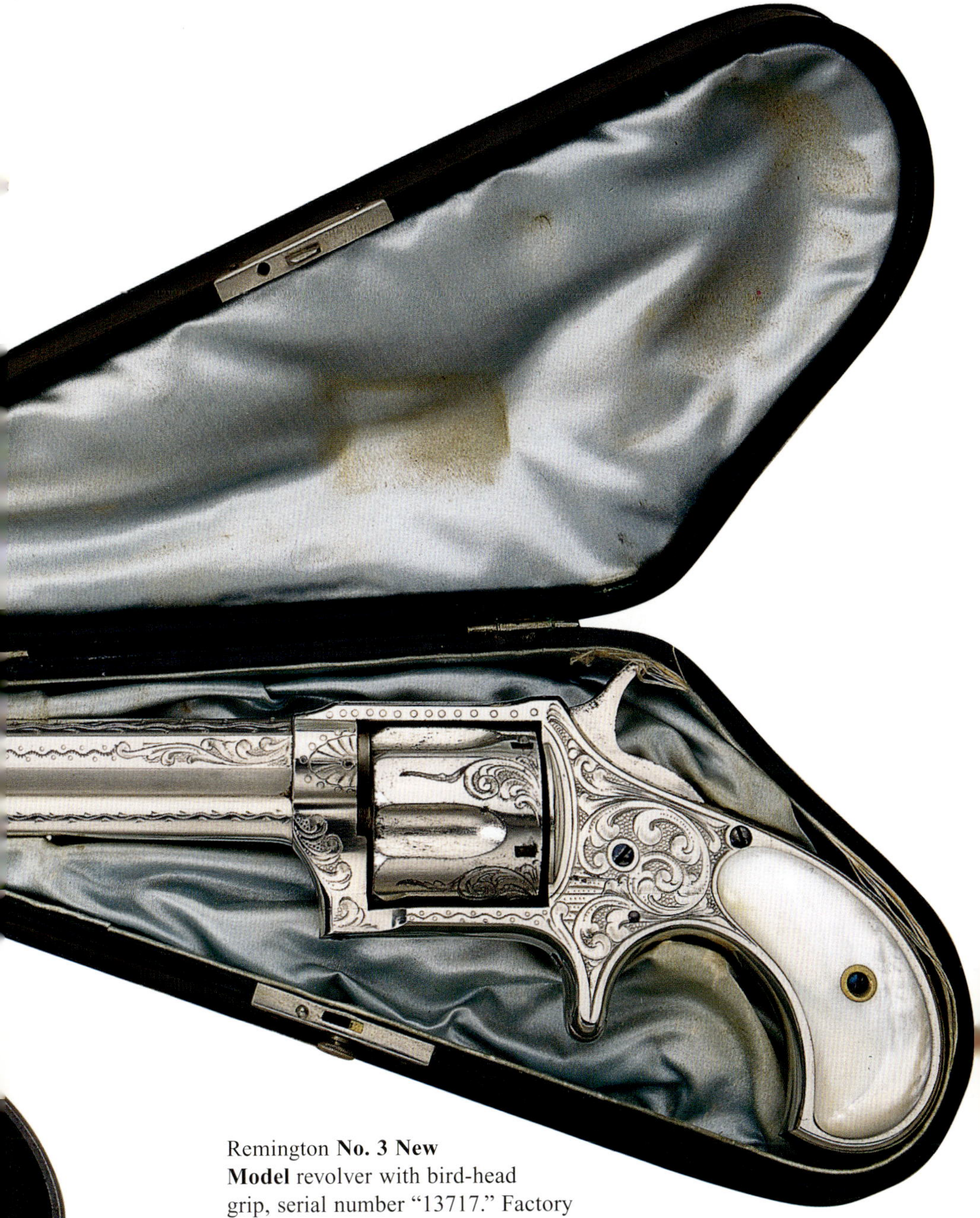

Remington **No. 3 New Model** revolver with bird-head grip, serial number "13717." Factory engraved and nickel plated, mother-of-pearl grips, octagonal barrel with large front sight. Caliber .38 rimfire. Pipe-style casing. *Photograph courtesy Paul Goodwin from* The Guns of Remington; *Gordon Stanley collection*

Remington **No. 3 New Model** revolver with saw handle grip, serial number "27409." Factory engraved and nickel plated, mother-of-pearl grips. Caliber .38 rimfire. *Photograph courtesy Paul Goodwin from* The Guns of Remington; *Robert J. Allen collection*

Remington **No. 4 New Model** revolver, serial number "8183." Factory engraved and nickel plated with gold washed cylinder and hammer, mother-of-pearl grips. Caliber .41 rimfire. *Photograph courtesy Paul Goodwin from* The Guns of Remington; *Randall W. Squire collection*

Table 1-D

Frequency of No. 1 RRS milling variations: cylinder bushing and cylinder chamber circles.

Revolving Recoil Shield Milling		
Serial # Interval N= 57	**Bushing on Cylinder**	**Circles on Cylinder Chambers**
001 -100	2	7
101-200	2	8
201-300	1	3
301-400	1	8
401-500	1	2
501 -600	3	1
601-700	3	2
TOTAL	13	31
PERCENTAGE	22.8%	54.4%

of the cylinder area. On the No. 1 with fixed recoil shield there is less beveling and a sharper, squared edge at this frame point (compare photo 1-01 with photo 1-07). A cartridge insertion flute in the right frame is $^{7}/_{16}$ inch long by $^{9}/_{32}$ inch wide, and is uniform on all No. 1 revolvers. This was essentially to aid in the loading and removal of cartridges. No other milling features were noted on the No. 1 revolver.

Recoil Shield

Because the patent description distinguishes the RRS feature, some discussion seems in order about its fundamental purpose. W.S. Smoot introduced this feature to control the possibility of firing a cartridge with too large a head, which could result in damage as well as extraction difficulties. The projection, or raised surface, found on the forward face of the shield prevented the cartridge head from reaching firing position (photos 1-07 and 1-01). Normally, this raised portion of the recoil shield would come directly behind the cartridge to be fired when the shield rotates to a down position (photo 1-01). That closed the opening through which cartridges were inserted. When the recoil shield was rotated in an upward direction, the cutout portion of the shield was then positioned for cartridge insertion (photo 1-11). A small spring recessed in the top frame strap engaged two notch points on the shield to hold it firmly in the two designated positions, *i.e.,* open and closed (photo 1-12). The spring must be depressed to remove it from the V-groove milled into the outer edge of the recoil shield. A small projection in the bottom frame serves to engage the groove and also stabilizes the rotations of the shield (photo 1-09).

There would appear to be some wisdom in perfecting a guard against faulty cartridges, and it would have been even more typical to incorporate such a safeguard during the early 1870s. The fact that cartridge manufacturers did not have effective quality control on cartridge sizes, powder, loading, ignition systems, and shell gauges led to difficulty with all kinds of firearms. Apparently, as cartridge manufacturing processes improved and as Remington gained production experience, the necessity for a revolving recoil shield diminished. Examination of this system led to the conclusion that additional milling operations and fitting were needed, which added to the revolver's cost. Moldenhauer, in a personal communication[20], observed that at least eight to ten separate milling operations would have been necessary for the RRS. Introduction of the fixed recoil shield made construction far simpler, and eliminated the problem of a

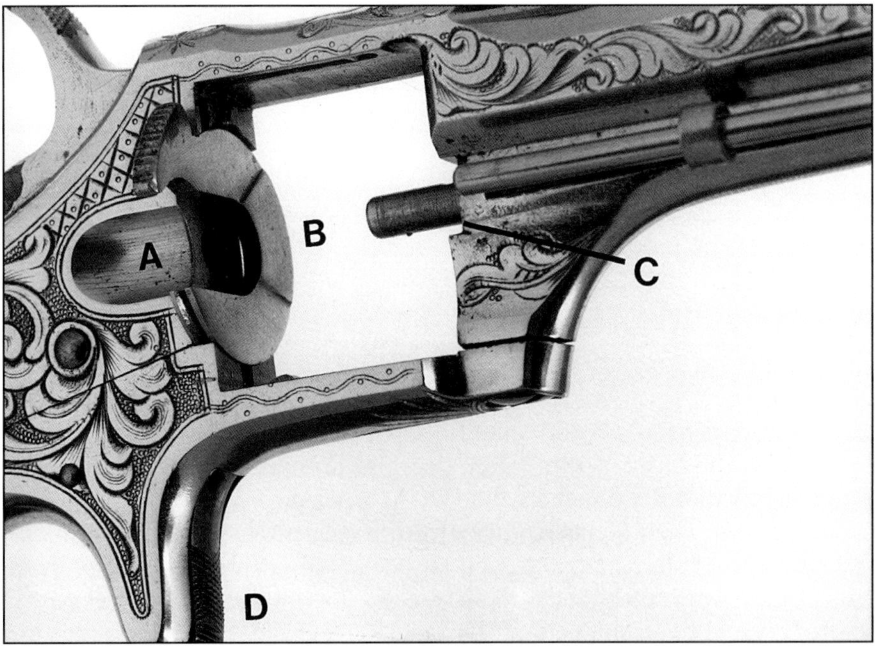

1-11. Detail view of right side of a No. 1 New Model revolver, showing revolving recoil shield (B) in up position for loading and ejecting shells through frame cut-out (A). Note cut-out in front of frame for cylinder bushing (C), and knurling on trigger face (D). *R.A. Cooper photograph*

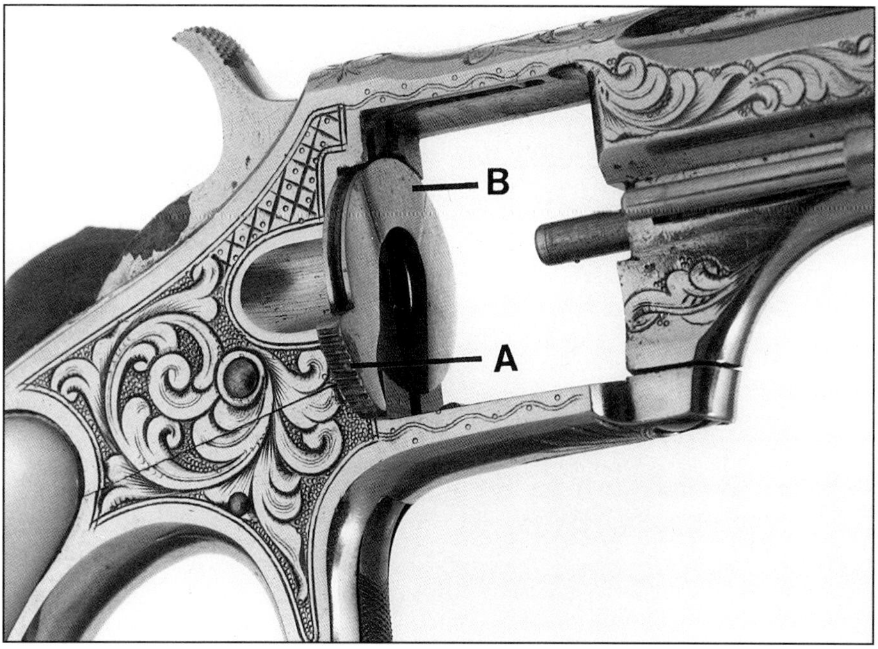

1-12. Detail view of right side of a No. 1 New Model revolver, showing revolving recoil shield (B) in down position for firing. Note raised surface on face of shield, designed to prevent cartridges with oversize heads from aligning into firing position. *R.A. Cooper photograph*

fragile spring and wear or damage to moving parts. Both factors, *i.e.*, more reliable cartridges and manufacturing economics, seem logical reasons for abandoning the revolving recoil shield and adopting the fixed type.

The decision to manufacture the No. 1 revolver, as well as the Nos. 2, 3, and 4 models, with a fixed recoil shield greatly improved the revolver's performance. This feature lessened the prospect of repairs and maintenance, and surely shortened production time by reducing extensive machining. An examination of the fixed recoil shield finds it secured to the frame by a screw (photo 1-07). The purpose of a raised portion on the forward face was to stop any cartridge with an oversized head. Thus, the same safety elements are present. But the revolving aspects requiring considerable additional machining were non-essential to performance.

Summary

The No. 1 revolver, having production of perhaps 3,000 units, was available only in .30 caliber, and in all finishes and grip materials normally offered by Remington. The change from a revolving recoil shield to a fixed one improved the revolver and made it less likely to require repair. The limitation of caliber size had much to do with its success, and probably influenced subsequent production of the No. 2 revolver in .32 caliber.

The presence of so many intact specimens supports the historical fact that William S. Smoot made a valuable contribution to the Remington reputation, and that his name and patent date justly belong on this uniquely fabricated revolver.

Notes:

1. Alden Hatch, *Remington Arms in American History*, p. 146.
2. Harold L. Peterson, *The Remington Historical Treasury of American Guns*, p. 54.
3. Harry J. Parker, "Remington Number 4 Revolver, New Model," in *Arms Gazette*, Vol. 2, No. 5, January 1974, p. 34.
4. *Public Auction of the Karl F. Moldenhauer Collection of Remington Arms*, p. 255. Hereafter cited as "*Moldenhauer Collection*."
5. Robert W.D. Ball, *Remington Firearms: The Golden Age of Collecting*, p. 128.
6. Charles L. Karr, Jr. and Carroll R. Karr, *Remington Handguns* (2nd edition), p. 78.
7. Jerry Landskron, *Remington Rolling Block Pistols*, p. 183.
8. Karr and Karr, p. 117.
9. G. Noether, *Introduction to Statistics: A Fresh Approach* (2nd edition), p. 2-6.
10. Jerrald H. Zar, *Biostatistical Analysis* (4th edition), pp. 462-466.
11. Noether, p. 30-32.
12. Karr and Karr, p. 140.
13. *Moldenhauer Collection*, p. 4.
14. Author's communication with Remington arms authority Karl F. Moldenhauer, 1970.
15. *Moldenhauer Collection,* p. 237.
16. W.J. Roff and J.R. Scott, *Handbook of Common Polymers*, p. 163.
17. James R. Somers, "The Remington New Line Revolvers," in *The Texas Gun Collector*, Vol. 59, June 1955, p. 22.
18. *Moldenhauer Collection*, p. 236.
19. *Ibid.*, pp. 236-237.
20. Author's communication with Remington arms authority Karl F. Moldenhauer, 1970.

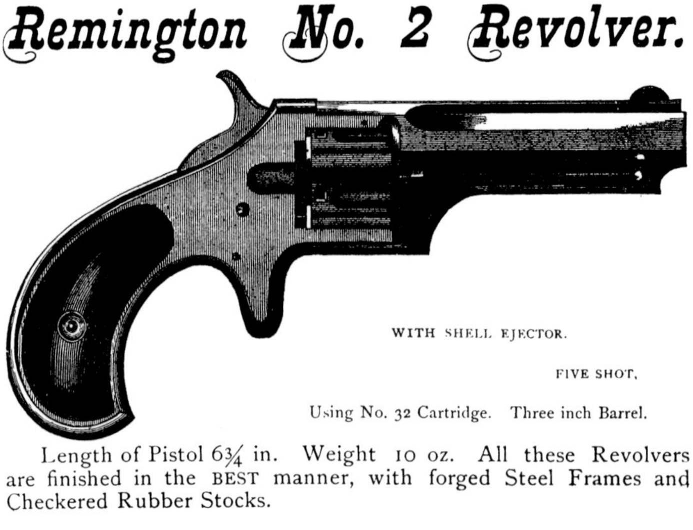

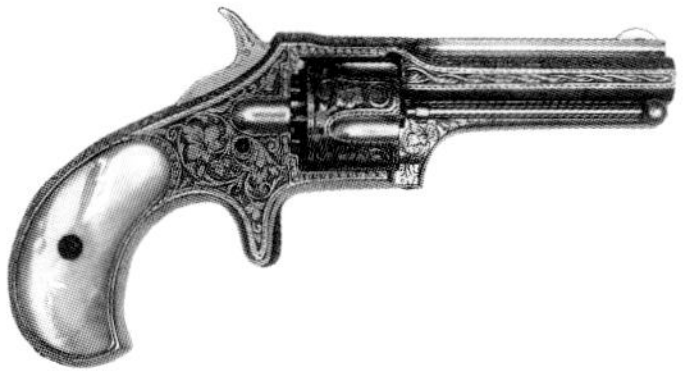

Chapter II

Remington Number 2 (Smoot's Patent) New Model Revolver

The senior author's initial venture into writing for gun collectors was in the *Wisconsin Gun Collector Annual* with an article on the No. 2 revolver.[1] That effort resulted in some key questions about Remington nomenclature. Curiously, beginning with the 1878 issue, when the No. 2 first appeared, Remington catalogs until 1885 displayed an engraving cut of the No. 1 revolver to represent the No. 2 model. Specific identifying features of the No. 1 are the revolving or fixed recoil shield, the "two-stepped" ejector rod, and the screw under the muzzle to retain the ejector rod. Although these features of the No. 1 revolver were clearly visible in the catalogs, the erroneous engraving was used in Remington publications for a number of years.

Of additional importance is the fact that gun collectors and arms dealers have frequently confused the No. 1 and No. 2 revolvers, unless specific details and measurements were known. For those individuals, .30 caliber identified the No. 1, and .32 caliber identified the No. 2. However as shall be seen later, caliber is not an exclusive criterion. Even though the No. 2 revolver was advertised only in .32 caliber, it actually was made in both .30 and .32 calibers. It is unclear why Karr and Karr[2] illustrated a No. 2 revolver (serial number "422") from the Remington Museum Collection as an example of the No. 1 revolver. Their error has misled many readers, collectors, and dealers into being unaware of the differences between the No. 1 and No. 2 revolvers, as noted above. Somers[3] identified some minor dimensional differences between the No. 1 and No. 2 revolvers, and was the first published credible reference to do so.

The No. 2 revolver first appeared in the October 1, 1878 factory catalog, along with models No. 1, 3, and 4. Karr and Karr[4] erroneously cite the initial manufacture date as 1874, with manufacture continuing until 1888. Factory catalogs for 1875, 1876, and 1877 do not show the No. 2, nor do they make any announcement of its eventual availability.

Serial Numbering

Serial Number Data

The No. 2 revolver was offered for sale in the Remington catalog along with other small pocket revolvers of similar caliber, and apparently it was a popular item that enjoyed a record of good sales. Many specimens exist today on which an estimate can be made about its overall production. Since availability of the No. 2 revolver was concurrent with other Smoot's Patent revolvers, it may easily be assumed that, as a distinct model, its serial numbering would begin with "1." Records reveal the existence of a specimen with serial number "1," while the highest number recorded to date is "2102." Up to serial number "1000" the authors have recorded specimens that were scattered by not more than fifteen to twenty digits. From serial "1001" and up, the differences in serial numbers were larger. In the first five intervals sixty-eight specimens in .30 caliber made up 87.2% of the sample. For .32 caliber, 157 recorded specimens made up 84.9% of the sample. The decline after serial number "1000" is obvious and suggests that production was minimal (see Table 2-A). In some cases, enough specimens have been seen and recorded to show a clustering and, frequently, an important serial number sequence and pattern.

Estimates of No. 2 Production

Over the last four decades, few specimens have been recorded beyond serial number "2000." Interestingly those examined since the early 1980s to the mid-nineties have almost uniformly fallen under serial number "2000." Certainly it can be said from the observed specimens, that 2,000 was the probable total number produced. In this sample only six revolvers were recorded with serial numbers beyond "2000." Nearly 260 (97.7% in the observed sample) were below the "2000" serial number range. Statistical treatment, based on the 263 observed specimens and statistical estimates of the total produced, places production at 2,127 with a 95% confidence factor.

No evidence exists to support the premise that Remington renumbered the No. 2 revolver. The production estimate of the authors, one tenth of that estimated by Karr and Karr[5], is credible. The authors of this volume consider their data more credible for the following reasons:

- Only six specimens have been found with serial numbers beyond "2000" (up to "2102"). The significant clustering falls within the "2000" range.
- No five-digit serial numbers have been found on any specimens to date, and none is known to exist. Considering the number of observations obtained, it is highly unlikely that a five-digit serial number would not be found if one exists.
- No duplicate number, nor any systematic plan or evidence of "batch" serial numbering, was observed suggestive of the large production that Karr and Karr estimated.[6]

Of all the Smoot's Patent revolvers recorded in this work, only the No. 2 has shown any duplicate-numbered specimens. In each case, these duplicate-

Table 2-A

No. 2 Revolver sample frequency for types of finish on .30 and .32 revolvers for all serial number intervals.

	Finish								
Serial No. Intervals	.30 Caliber				.32 Caliber				
	Nickel	Blue	Engraved	Total	Nickel	Blue	Engraved	Unknown	Total
001 - 200	13		1	14	22	2	8	1	33
201 - 400	11	1	2	14	20		10	1	31
401 - 600	14		2	16	23	2	4		29
601 - 800	11		2	13	20	1	7		28
801 - 1000	10		1	11	23		10		33
1001 - 1200	2			2	8		3		11
1201 - 1400	2			2	3		2		5
1401 - 1600	1			1	5		1	1	7
1601 - 1800					4	1			5
1801 - 2000	3		1	4	1				1
2001 - 2200	1			1	4		1		5
TOTAL	68	1	9	78	133	6	46	3	188
Percentage	87.2%	1.3%	11.5%		71.9%	3.2%	24.9%		

*Not included in this table: Gold and mixed-finish specimens.

numbered pieces clearly differed in quality of finish, caliber, and grips. Of the fourteen pairs of duplicates, ten had one of the pair different in finish, and in seven of the pairs, one of the pair was of a different caliber. Only two pairs (serial numbers "213" and "418") of the fourteen had similar finish and caliber; however, recorded details such as grip material or finish quality distinguished even these pairs. In fact, serial number "977" is a unique, distinctly engraved piece, finished in gold with pearl grips and cased (photo 2-01 and in color on page 45, right). Its serial number mate is a mint, nickel plated, .30 caliber rubber gripped revolver in its original box, formerly in the Moldenhauer Collection.[7] This duplication reflects what must be regarded as production errors.

Serial Number Location and Stamping Practice

All serial number stamping is found under the left grip on both parts of the frame. Thus, the serial number appears twice and is adjacent to the frame joint (photo 2-02). Several specimens have been examined with mixed serial numbers. One specimen has "279" on the top frame and "368" on the bottom frame. The fact that it is factory engraved and with a gold washed hammer led to the conclusion that it is an authentic specimen with a factory numbering error.

Serial numbers were not stamped elsewhere on the revolver, and the factory practice was consistent in this regard. Other stampings, such as single digits or letter symbols, have been found on the recoil shield, on the top and bottom straps, and on the cylinder. Serial number "871" has the number "4" on the recoil shield and on the back of the cylinder (photo 2-03). These digits appear to be an assembly coding, since they bear no relationship to the serial number of the specimen. Serial number "1206" shows an "H"-like symbol on the strap.

No specimen of the No. 2 revolver has been examined that is without a serial number. However, other models of Smoot's Patent revolvers have been studied in which numerous specimens had no serial numbers. The lack of specimens without numbers makes it obvious that serial numbering was standard practice on the No. 2 revolver.

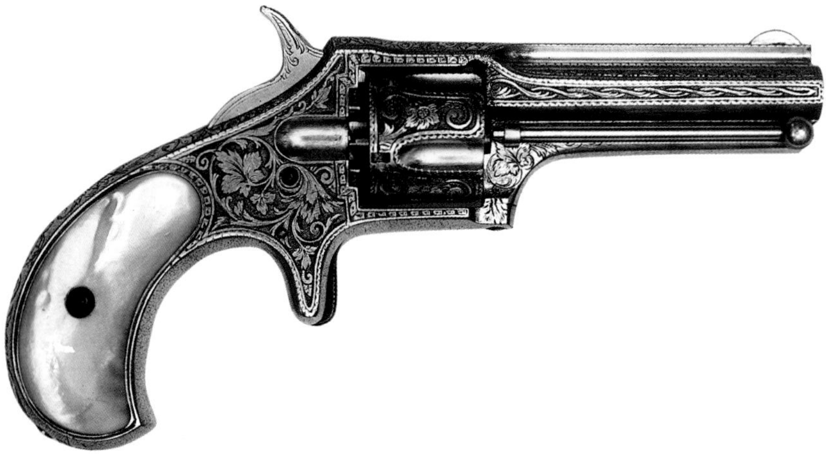

2-01. Remington No. 2 New Model revolver, having profuse factory engraving of a type done on special order, serial number "977." Overall gold washed, mother-of-pearl grips. *R.A. Cooper photograph*

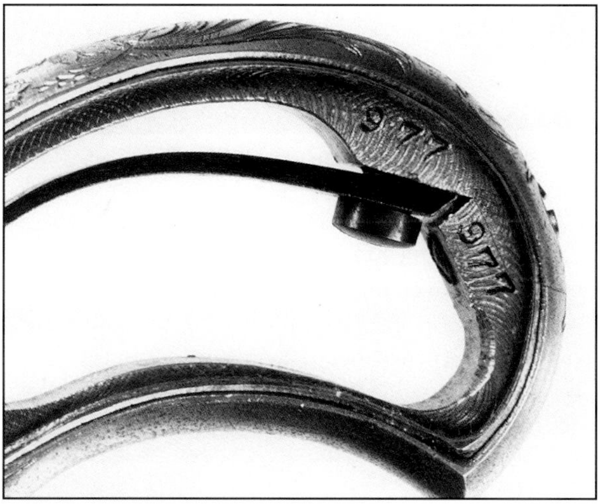

2-02. (Left) Detail view, showing serial number locations on left side of top and bottom frame halves. *R.A. Cooper photograph*

2-03. (Below) Detail view of right side of a No. 2 New Model revolver, showing assembly number "4" on recoil shield and crosshatch pattern on trigger face distinctive to this model. *R.A. Cooper photograph*

Identifying Features of the Model No. 2

Caliber Data

While a catalog of the period cites .32 as the designated caliber, many No. 2 revolvers have appeared in .30 caliber. Karr and Karr failed to note this, although Somers[8] did. Nearly 31% of the specimens in the sample were in .30 caliber (see Table 2-A). As noted earlier, gun dealers have frequently misclassified the No. 2 revolver in .30 caliber as the No. 1 model, since the two are similar. Both Somers and Parker[9] have pointed out the significant distinction between these two models.

The Remington Museum has an engraved specimen (serial number "422") in .30 caliber, so this caliber does exist legitimately. The sample shows no spread of numbers allotted to .30 caliber designation. What does appear is an apparent random pattern, suggesting that throughout the probably two thousand or more revolvers produced, those in .30 caliber were bored per request or by management decision.

With regard to the serial numbers of No. 2 revolvers in .30 caliber, serial number "1" was the lowest recorded, with a high incidence up to serial "1000." The limited number from "1001" to "2102" precludes any inferences about the magnitude or pattern of caliber designation. As we have noted, serial numbers decreased above "1000." Specimens in .30 caliber recorded up to serial number "1000" accounted for 31% of production. For .32 caliber, the 68% recorded amounts to over twice that of the .30 caliber. Also, a minimal number were observed in the intervals from "1001" to "2200." For both calibers, 77% of those observed bore serial number "1000" or lower. The No. 2 revolver was made in .30 caliber within its initial production run, while the No. 1 revolver was still being advertised for sale. This has been borne out by the serial number data and by the Remington catalogs of the period. A review of the sample serial number data in Table 2-A reveals that of the 263 revolvers observed, 19.6% were in .30 caliber. In the intervals, only nine revolvers out of the thirty-eight sampled were recorded in .30 caliber. The distribution in Table 2-A indicates that observed pieces in both .30 and .32 calibers dropped off significantly after serial number interval "1000."

Clearly, the .32 caliber was predominant, accounting for seven out of ten recorded. The three unknown caliber specimens represent a negligible sampling matter. One non-Remington modification was present. For the .32 caliber revolvers recorded, Table 2-A indicates that it, too, experienced a decline in occurrence, and thus production, after serial number "1000." In particular, the sampling after serial "1000" was notably limited with six specimens, only one of which was in .30 caliber.

Curiously, catalogs of the period indicate that .32 caliber was the only bore for the No. 2 revolver. Apparently, a retailer had to special order .30 caliber. To date no factory specimen has been examined, or is known to exist, in a caliber other than .30 or .32.

Finishes

Catalogs of the period indicate that the No. 2 revolver could be had in nickel plate, blue, engraved, or specially plated finishes (see Table 2-A). Nickel plate was clearly the common or popular finish of the day. Of the specimens observed in both calibers 76% had nickel finish. For .30 caliber, nickel plate was recorded for 87.2% in all intervals, while .32 caliber accounted for 71.9%. In reviewing the differences, or trends by intervals, Table 2-A notes that for serial number intervals "1" to "600," nickel represents 86.4% of the .30 caliber and

71.6% of the .32 caliber specimens. In serial number intervals "601" through "1000," nickel plate represents 87.5% for .30 caliber, a slight increase from the initial intervals. For .32 caliber, 64.7% of these intervals represented a decrease from the initial intervals. For the intervals up to serial "2000," the 87% nickel plate in .30 caliber was similar to that of the initial intervals. For .32 caliber, 71.7% was nearly comparable to initial intervals.

Blue finish specimens were clearly scarce, representing only 2.6% of the sample for both calibers. Only seven blue specimens have been recorded in the sample, one of which was in .30 caliber. Blue specimens were recorded in the intervals below serial number "800," a limited incidence similar to that found for the No. 1 revolver. Only one specimen in .32 caliber was recorded in serial number intervals "1601" to "1800." Although other revolvers in the Remington catalog were available in the well-known blue finish, it is not known why so few have been recorded for the No. 2 revolver. Catalogs reveal that blue finish was slightly cheaper than nickel plate. This suggests that some factor other than cost affected customer choice of finish.

Engraved specimens in the sample represent 20.7% for both calibers (see Table 2-A). Five times as many were recorded for .32 than for .30 caliber. In the serial number intervals up to "1000," both calibers represented 11.7% of the sample. Up to serial number "2000," 11.1% of the .30 caliber specimens were engraved. All finishes reflected the reduction as availability declined. Engraved specimens in .32 caliber showed 24.2% in the initial intervals up to serial number "600." There was an increase in incidence from serial number "601" to "1000." For the same intervals, .32 caliber showed three times the incidence compared with .30 caliber. For serial numbers "1001" to "2000," a reduction to 21.4% occurred in the sample, a level closer to the occurrences of the first 600 serial numbers for .32 caliber.

With respect to engraving, Remington did not appear to use levels or grades, or to even provide customers with sample sketches of an engraved gun (photo 2-05). More surprising is the fact that Remington never published an engraving cut in any of its catalogs. Certainly, sales might have been increased by such publication. Evaluating the number of engraved specimens for the No. 2 revolver, it became apparent that it was similar to the No. 1 in many aspects. The engraving style, the surfaces involved, the quality of detail and the incidence all led to the conclusion that what was found for the No. 1 revolver applies equally to the No. 2.

Particularly noteworthy is the incidence of mixed-finish specimens recorded in this sample. These were engraved revolvers with gold or blue on their various parts. Some specimens were recorded that were not engraved but that had gold washed parts, *e.g.*, cylinder or ejector rod. Again, the catalogs and advertising price lists provide no information regarding either gilt or gold plating. Even the terms "gold wash" or "gold plate" were not defined in the catalogs. Other arms manufacturers used silver as a specially plated finish; there-

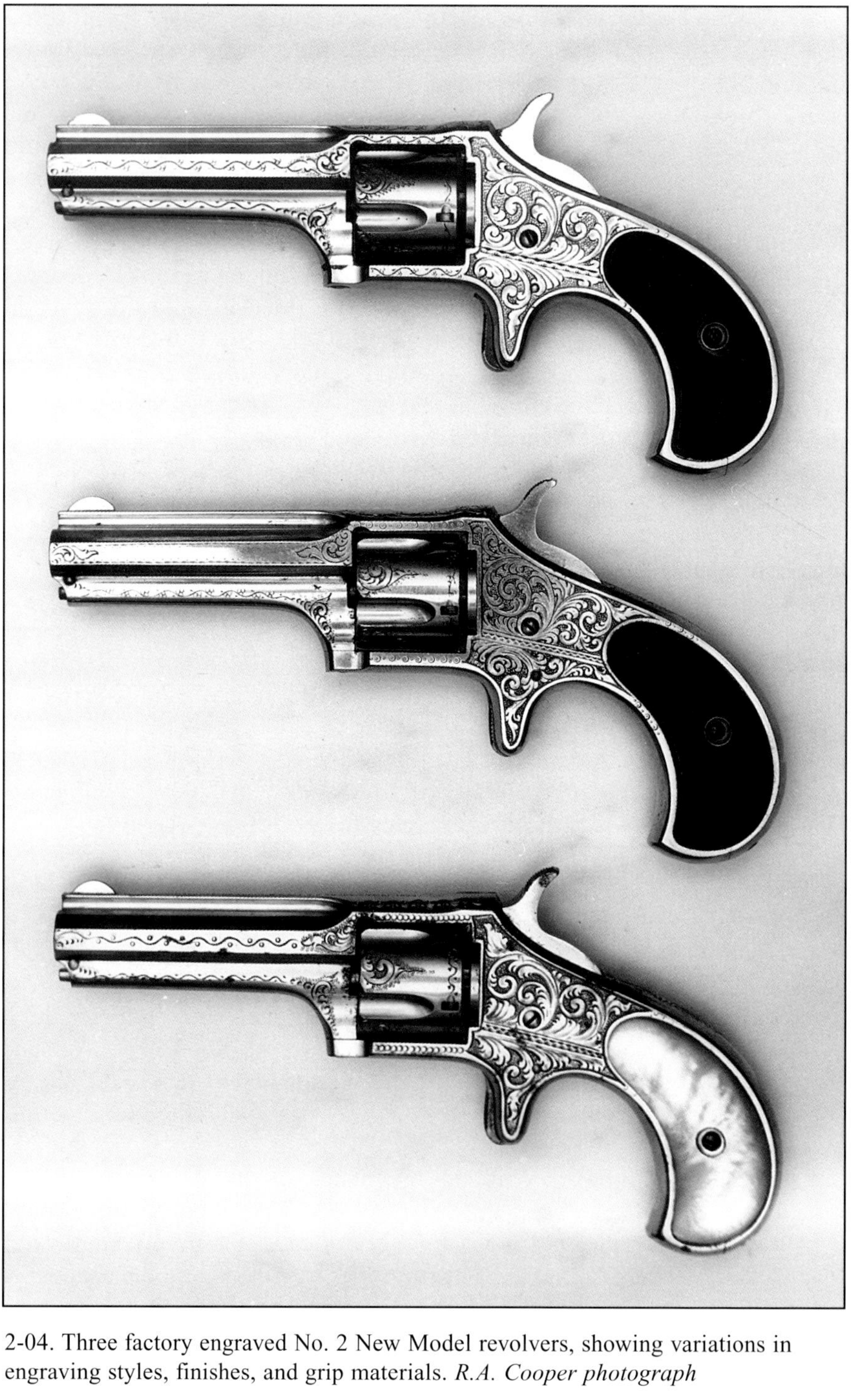

2-04. Three factory engraved No. 2 New Model revolvers, showing variations in engraving styles, finishes, and grip materials. *R.A. Cooper photograph*

fore, it seems reasonable to assume that Remington also provided it on request. However, no such specimen has been recorded for the No. 2 sample.

While the preceding discussion identified caliber and finish differences, Table 2-A provides interval specifics for .30 and .32 calibers. Summarizing to this point, nickel was found on 87% of the .30 caliber specimens, and on 72% of those in .32 caliber; 76% were nickel for both calibers. Engraved specimens in .32 caliber were five times more evident than those recorded for .30 caliber. Blue finish was noticeably scarce, with only one specimen recorded in .30 caliber and six in .32 caliber.

When Table 2-A sampling distribution by caliber is examined, entries recorded per serial number interval initially are relatively similar for both calibers up to serial number "1000." Thereafter, serial numbers dropped off to less than ten per interval. This conveys the possibility of a Remington reduction in production and its resulting impact on sales.

From serial "1001" to "2000," the incidence for .30 caliber was nine specimens. This suggests that availability diminished for any specimen with a serial number in these intervals. A similar portrait is revealed for .32 caliber, its incidence per interval approximately double that of .30 caliber. This is consistent with evidence that the production of .32 caliber specimens exceeded that of .30 caliber specimens by a factor of two or more.

2-05. Detail view of top surfaces of two No. 2 New Model revolvers, showing patent date in barrel marking, rear sights, and hammer knurling. *R.A. Cooper photograph*

Types of Grips

The No. 2 revolver first appeared in the October 1878 Remington factory catalog. Only pearl and ivory grips were listed as available, with prices given for each. There were no listings available indicating that wood or checkered hard rubber grips could be provided in lieu of pearl or ivory. Since Remington had offered wood grips on other models for some time, it seems strange that the No. 2 sample had so few specimens with wood grips. Table 2-B shows the serial number intervals, with only six examples having walnut grips and one with rosewood, comprising 2.6% of the entire sample. All were in .32 caliber.

Of the entire sample, the forty-two specimens with pearl grips represent 15.8% of the grip materials. Pearl was also more expensive than Remington "ivory." In the sample, five .30 caliber specimens, or 6.4%, were in pearl, while 20% of the thirty-seven specimens in .32 caliber had grips of pearl. For both calibers in intervals up to serial number "1000," 14% were in pearl. Most engraved pieces had pearl grips, although occasionally engraved revolvers appeared with rubber grips (photo 2-04). It cannot be determined what kind of grips these revolvers were equipped with when originally shipped from Remington.

As previously discussed relative to the No. 1 revolver model, the Remington "ivory" grips were, in fact, made of a plasticized nitrocellulose product named "celluloid," which was used specifically to imitate real ivory. This type of celluloid grip represented 7.9% of the sample for twenty-one specimens recorded in both calibers. Table 2-B shows three times the number of .32 caliber revolvers with Remington celluloid as were found in the .30 caliber sample. The vast majority of Remington celluloid grips were identified with serial numbers under "1000." Table 2-B indicates that only three (1.1%) specimens having genuine ivory grips have been recorded, all in .32 caliber with serial numbers under "1000." Apparently Remington did respond to customers who requested genuine ivory. It seems misleading, if not outright deceptive, that the company did not make clear the distinction in its catalogs.

It is clear that checkered hard rubber comprised the grip material for 70.7% of the entire sample. Of the sixty-six .30 caliber specimens, 84.6% were so equipped. Nearly twice that number (122, or 65.9%) were in .32 caliber. Serial number intervals up to "1000" made up a preponderance (83%) of the specimens. While the vast majority of hard rubber grips were of a dark, even jet-black rubber, some specimens were dark brown. Other grips were noted with a lighter black, verging on grayish, color.

The effects of advertising for grips made of pearl and ivory in catalogs and price lists suggest that a paradoxical response occurred when the observed data were evaluated. The initial lack of advertising for wood or checkered hard rubber suggests that rubber was the "standard" grip material for revolvers. Nothing conveyed the fact that wood was similarly viewed, even though Remington's history with other models supports a high incidence in the use of wood

Table 2-B

No. 2 revolver sample frequency for types of grip materials on .30 and .32 revolvers for all serial number intervals.

.30 Caliber							
Serial # Intervals	1 Walnut	3 Pearl	4 Rem. Cell.	6 Chkr. Rubber	7 Sm. Rubber	8 Unknown	Total
001 - 200			2	11	1		14
201 - 400		1		13			14
401 - 600		1		14		1	16
601 - 800		2	1	10			13
801 - 1000			1	10			11
1001 - 1200			1	1			2
1201 - 1400				2			2
1401 - 1600				1			1
1601 - 1800							0
1801 - 2000		1		3			4
2001 - 2200				1			1
TOTAL		5	5	66	1	1	78
Percentage		6.4%	6.4%	84.6%	1.3%	1.3%	

.32 Caliber							
Serial # Intervals	1 Walnut	2 Rose.	3 Pearl	4 Rem. Cell.	5 Real Ivory	6 Chkr. Rubber	Total
001 - 200	1		9	5		17	32
201 - 400	2	1	6	4	1	16	30
401 - 600			5	1		23	29
601 - 800			4	2	1	21	28
801 - 1000	1		9	2	1	20	33
1001 - 1200			1	1		9	11
1201 - 1400			1			4	5
1401 - 1600	1		1			4	6
1601 - 1800				1		4	5
1801 - 2000	1						1
2001 - 2200			1			4	5
TOTAL	6	1	37	16	3	122	185
Percentage	3.2%	0.5%	20%	8.6%	1.6%	65.9%	

1. Walnut 2. Rosewood 3. Pearl 4. Rem Celluloid 5. Real Ivory 6. Checkered Rubber 7. Smooth Rubber 8. Unknown

as a grip material. The grip experience with the No. 1 revolver led to a similar response in marketing the No. 2 model.

Hammer, Trigger, Springs, and Screws

For these four components, the experiences and data on specific detail found for the No. 1 revolver apply similarly to the No. 2 model. The reader is directed to those items as presented in Chapter I.

Markings

All of the commentary on markings found for the No. 1 Smoot's Patent revolver applies similarly to the No. 2 revolver.

Sights

Front sights for the No. 2 revolver are essentially the same in all respects as those found on the No. 4 revolver. The No. 2 rear sight was likewise identical in milling to that of the No. 1 (photo 2-05).

Barrel and Frame Assembly

Following the experience and detail of the No. 1 revolver, Remington repeated the dimensions and machining techniques on the No. 2 revolver. As was the case with the No. 1 model, the merit of machining so many elements with the barrel, many of which were subject to production errors and related costs, remains a mystery. The bottom part of the frame shows less evident machining or finishing than the top frame, even though it houses the trigger elements (photo 2-06). Here the trigger, its flat spring, screw, cylinder bolt, and drift pin represent the elements in the small portion of the frame. Restating an earlier observation, it is unclear what caused Remington to produce a revolver with so many complex milling operations. However, on balance, one cannot fault the assembly in either design or operation as being unsafe, frail, or inaccessible for maintenance.

Cylinder Center Pin and Shell Ejection System

Remington repeated the use of the cylinder pin and shell ejection system found in the No. 1 as part of its unique patent features. For the No. 2 revolver, the ejector rod evolved into one with a single circumference 2½ inches long by $^{3}/_{32}$ inch in diameter. With the No. 2, this simplified the milling or lathe work necessary, making for less expense. This change became an obvious identifying feature for the No. 2 revolver. The rod's single circumference did not prevent excessive compression by the user. Rough handling in ejection could limit the spring tension needed to keep the rod at the muzzle-forward position. Thus, the same problems found in the No. 1 revolver could manifest themselves with the No. 2. Surprisingly, no change was made in either the metal gauge or quality of the spring.

Another identifying element that distinguishes the No. 2 from the No. 1 is the cross pin under the muzzle, which retains the ejector rod in the channel web. While milling screw threads requires more production time and effort, removing a screw would seem easier to do than removing the pin. Drilling a hole for a drift pin was easier in production, but required the proper size punch for removal by a customer.

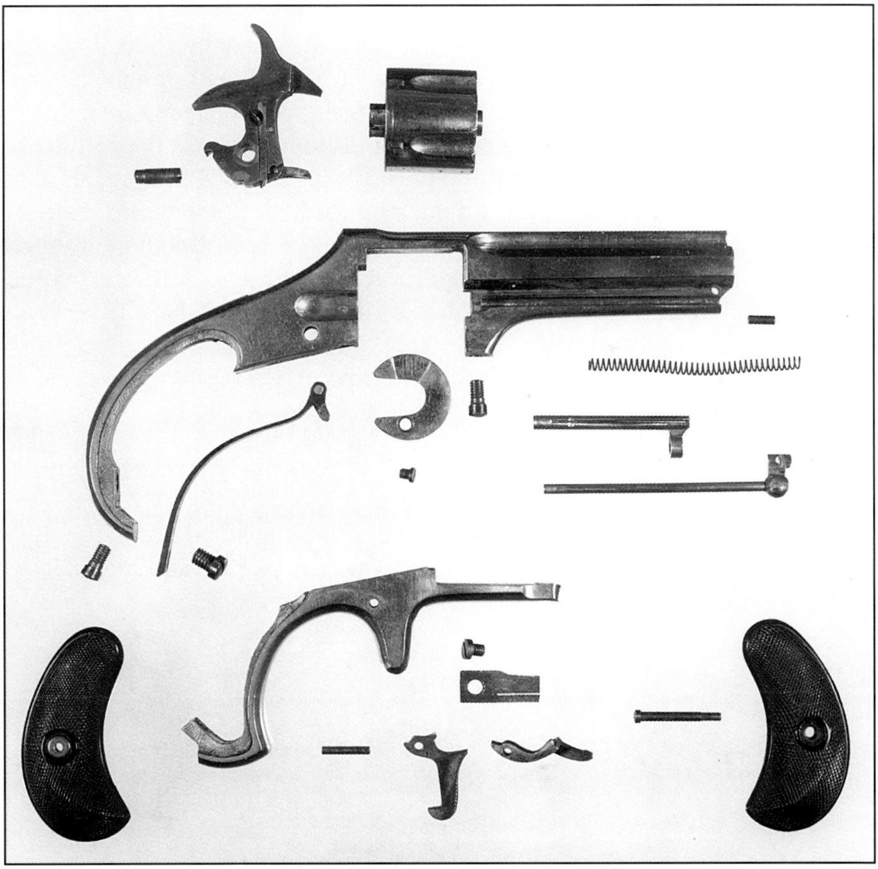

2-06. Disassembled view of a No. 2 New Model revolver, showing component parts: upper and lower frame halves, hammer, cylinder, recoil shield, ejector rod, cylinder pin, mainspring and ejector spring, grips, and miscellaneous internal parts.
R.A. Cooper photograph

Bushings, Cylinder, Milling, and Recoil Shield

These elements were covered in the No. 1 revolver discussion, and apply here as well. Cylinder length measurement for the No. 2 revolver is 7/8 inch, and is generally uniform for five-shot revolvers. Variations have been noted between .30 and .32 caliber specimens, with some varying from .875 to .901 inch in length. These variations were not regarded as important, nor seen as production variations. All cylinders have five flutes 5/8 inch long by ¼ inch wide. Cylinder stop notches are uniform, and no variations have been seen. Milling for the No. 2 right frame flute measures 19/32 inch long by 3/8 inch wide, and is uniform on all No. 2 revolvers. These dimensions were designed for ease of loading and for the ejection of shells. No other milling features have been noted on the No. 2 revolver.

The No. 2 revolver has a fixed recoil shield that follows the same style, dimensions, and details found on the No. 1 revolver. Karr and Karr noted that the first No. 2 revolvers were made with revolving recoil shields, and that later ones have fixed recoil shields.[10] This meant that the No. 2 revolver repeated the pattern of the No. 1 revolver, and its recoil shield change. No evidence or reference was offered by the authors, and nothing was found in Remington catalogs of the period to support their view. The senior author of the present work has never seen or recorded a No. 2 revolver with a revolving recoil shield. Remington's experience with the No. 1 revolving recoil shield manufacturing process and the transition to a fixed shield makes it unlikely that they reverted to those experiences by incorporating a revolving shield into production of the No. 2 revolver.

Summary

The No. 2 revolver was produced in both .30 and .32 calibers, with perhaps 2,127 guns manufactured. Compared to the No. 1, the No. 2 model is easily distinguished by its single circumference ejector rod, and cross pin under the muzzle which retains the ejector rod and spring. Among small frame Remington models, the No. 2 revolver appears frequently at gun shows and in collections, suggesting that it was indeed a popular sidearm.

Notes:

1. Harry J. Parker, "Remington Number 2 Revolver," in the *Third Annual Wisconsin Gun Collector*, 1964, pp. 25-30.
2. Charles L. Karr, Jr. and Carroll R. Karr, *Remington Handguns* (2nd edition), 1951, p. 110.
3. James R. Somers, "The Remington New Line Revolvers," in *The Texas Gun Collector*, Vol. 59, June 1955, p. 22.
4. Karr and Karr, p. 119.
5. *Ibid.*, p. 119.
6. *Ibid.*, pp. 139-142.
7. *Public Auction of the Karl F. Moldenhauer Collection of Remington Arms,* 1980, p. 245.
8. Somers, p. 22.
9. Harry J. Parker, "Remington Number 2 Revolver, New Model (Smoot's Patent) Part 1," in *Arms Gazette*, Vol. 3, No. 7, March 1976, pp. 10-14.
10. Karr and Karr, p. 81.

Chapter III

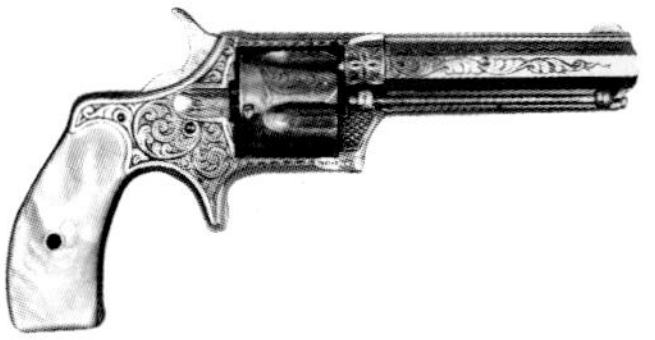

Remington Number 3 (Smoot's Patent) New Model Revolver

For the "bird-head" and "saw handle" versions (both names were derived from the shape of the grip frame, and are not known to have originated with Remington), the No. 3 revolver was also called a "Smoot." This derived largely from the fact that it contains the "Smoot's Patent" designation on the barrel. The use of the Smoot name as shorthand has been observed in advertisements by gun dealers and collectors who used it in their communications. The 1878 Remington catalog showed the No. 3 bird-head variation offered for sale with no "Smoot's Patent," "Smoot," or "New Line" designation, but with only the "New Model" designation following the title. Catalogs discussed here were only those produced by E. Remington & Sons having the Ilion, New York imprint.

While Karr and Karr indicate the dates of manufacture as 1875 to 1888[1], catalogs of the period reveal the No. 3 bird-head gripped, octagon-shaped barrel (BHO) first appeared in 1878. It is not found in catalogs after 1881. In fact, the saw handle variation was shown for the first time in the 1882 catalog, and also was termed the "No. 3 Revolver, New Model." Again Karr and Karr cite the same manufacturing dates. Of importance is the fact that the 1882 catalog neither pictures nor provides any explanation as to the availability of the BHO variation, or if it still was being offered for sale. More importantly, the description accompanying the No. 3 saw handle variation gives no hint of a new revolver being offered, or even that it was in any way a production variation. It may be speculated that catalogs were not meant to be the sole criterion as to what pieces were being manufactured currently, or were still for sale. In the absence of any manufacturing records, only a rough estimate is possible regarding production life made on the basis of catalog coverage.

The lack of specific records represents the primary difficulty in Remington arms research, as fires and general record destruction affect the availability of data. The categorization of serial number, finish, milling, caliber, grip material, and other distinguishing features represents the basis for describing the No. 3 revolver to the gun collecting fraternity. The following discussion is divided into three parts: the No. 3 bird-head, octagon barrel variation (BHO); the No. 3 bird-head, top ribbed barrel variation (BHR); and the No. 3 saw handle variation (SH).

Number 3 Bird-Head, Octagon Barrel (BHO) Revolver

It should be noted that the No. 3 revolver offered for sale in the 1878 catalog was a bird-head gripped, octagon barrel (BHO) with a small sight (photo 3-01, bottom), offered in five-shot, .38 caliber centerfire or rimfire calibers. Clearly, this was a larger pistol than the Smoot's Patent Nos. 1 or 2, and while machining, fabrication, and grip frame shape suggest similarities, the BHO is a distinct revolver. The separate barrel fabrication, the modified ejector and cylinder pin system, and its size distinguish this piece from the Smoot's Patent Nos. 1 and 2 revolvers.

3-01. A pair of Remington No. 3 New Model revolvers, showing octagonal barrels, bird-head grips, nickel plating and hard rubber grips (top), rare blue finish and Remington "ivory" (celluloid) grips (bottom). *R.A. Cooper photograph*

Serial Number Data

As has been observed in firearms research, one might assume logic would prompt assignment of a new sequence of numbers for a new revolver. Remington, like other arms manufacturers, occasionally did assign serial numbers in an articulated fashion, that is, continuing in order from an older manufactured model to a newer model. Remington appears to be no different from other manufacturers, in that the use of serial numbers was to serve the manufacturer's purposes rather than intended for the benefit of the public, the government, or law enforcement. Thus, decoding the assignment of serial numbers, the determination of serial number ranges, the occasional mixed sampling, and a lack of numbers on some revolvers all complicate the reconstruction of production records within a specific time frame, and affect the understanding of the variations observed.

Estimates of No. 3 BHO Production

Serial numbering for the BHO appeared to begin at "1005," which was the lowest serial number recorded. Of the one hundred or more revolvers recorded over the years, all have been above this value. The highest serial number recorded for the BHO variation was "15513" (see Table 3-A). Records of serial numbers show that for the range "1005" to "15513" gaps or breaks between many series were larger than several hundred. It therefore appears that the BHO revolver had a production life of some 12,000 pieces.

Statistical Treatment

Based on the recorded specimens up to serial number "15513," a statistical maximum of 14,417 was established with a 95% confidence factor. Karr and Karr indicated that for the BHO and the saw handle, total production was "estimated at over 25,000 for both types."[2]

Table 3-A presents the BHO serial number intervals and observed number of recorded specimens. Examination of each interval finds one (serial numbers "11001" through "12000") with no specimens recorded. Only a single specimen was recorded for intervals "1001" through "3000" and "15001" to "17000." Three intervals ("7001" to "9000," "9001" to "11000," and "13001" to "15000") recorded a two-digit frequency totaling fifty-three specimens, or 85.5% of the sample distribution. Clustering in the samples appeared in the intervals "7001" through "9000," consisting of eighteen specimens (29%), and "13001" through "15000" made up of twenty-four specimens (38.7%) for a total of 67.7% of the sample distribution.

The senior author has continued to search out specimens, recording serial numbers and descriptive information. There is no evidence that Remington

Table 3-A

No. 3 bird-head octagon barrel sample frequency for caliber, finish and grip material for all serial number intervals.

		Caliber		Finish		
Serial No. Intervals	Frequency	Rimfire	Centerfire	Nickel	Blue	Engraved
1001 - 3000	1	1		1		
3001 - 5000	5	4	1	3	1	1
5001 - 7000	2	2		2		
7001 - 9000	18	18		12	2	4
9001 - 11,000	11	4	7	7	3	1
11,001 - 13,000						
13,001 - 15,000	24	4	20	19		5
15,001 - 17,000	1	1			1	
TOTAL	62	34	28	44	7	11
Percentage		54.8%	45.2%	70.9%	11.3%	17.7%

	Grip Material							
Serial No. Intervals	1 Walnut	2 Rose.	3 Pearl	4 Cell.	5 Ivory	6 Chkr. Rubber	7 Sm. Rubber	8 Unknown
1001 - 3000						1		
3001 - 5000				1		4		
5001 - 7000						2		
7001 - 9000		1	2	2		13		
9001 - 11,000			1	5		5		
11,001 - 13,000								
13,001 - 15,000			1	3		20		
15,001 - 17,000						1		
TOTAL		1	4	11		46		
Percentage		1.6%	6.4%	17.7%		74.2%		

1. Walnut 2. Rosewood 3. Pearl 4. Celluloid 5. Ivory 6. Checkered Rubber 7. Smooth Rubber 8. Unknown

*Not included in this table: Gold and mixed-finish specimens.

used repetitive or "batch" serial numbering with the No. 3 BHO variation. Sufficient physical data for each revolver recorded would establish whether a specific piece was noted earlier. Over the years, specimens have been identified at gun shows as having belonged to different owners. When serial number ranges were reviewed, the pattern was limited in relationship to caliber. Records reveal that .38 centerfire caliber revolvers appear to have been located within serial numbers "9287" to "9842" and "13270" to "15000." All other revolvers were in .38 rimfire caliber. No relationship or pattern was discerned between serial number ranges and types of finish.

Serial Number Location and Stamping Practice

Serial number placement for the BHO has uniformly been found in two places: at the top and bottom strap enclosing the cylinder area (photo 3-02). In both locations the cylinder must be removed in order to read the serial numbers. Removal of screws retaining both parts of the frame also exposes the serial numbers.

Contrary to the note in Karr and Karr[3], no specimens have been examined bearing serial numbers elsewhere on a standard production revolver. Occasionally a specimen has been noted bearing single digits on the grip frame or on the back of the cylinder. This has been interpreted as a type of assembly coding, since these revolvers also have their serial numbers stamped in the proper location.

Only rarely has a BHO specimen been examined that bore no serial number. These are assumed to have been a salesman's sample, a factory theft, or perhaps a revolver removed from production because of a flaw.

Identifying Features of the No. 3 BHO Revolver

Caliber Data

The 1878 Remington catalog indicated that the BHO was available in .38 centerfire or rimfire calibers, and indicated, "the Center-Fire shells can be reloaded, thus reducing the cost of ammunition." Apparently, Remington was attempting to encourage the purchase of centerfire arms and ammunition for them.

In Table 3-A, an analysis of the serial number intervals for caliber distinctions finds twenty-eight specimens (45.2%) in centerfire. Thirty-four specimens in .38 rimfire found in the distribution represented 54.8% of the sample. Thus, Remington's attempt to encourage customers to use centerfire ammunition can be classified as having met only with modest success. No specimen has been inspected in a caliber other than those described above. Certainly, no production run involved calibers other than those found advertised in the catalogs.

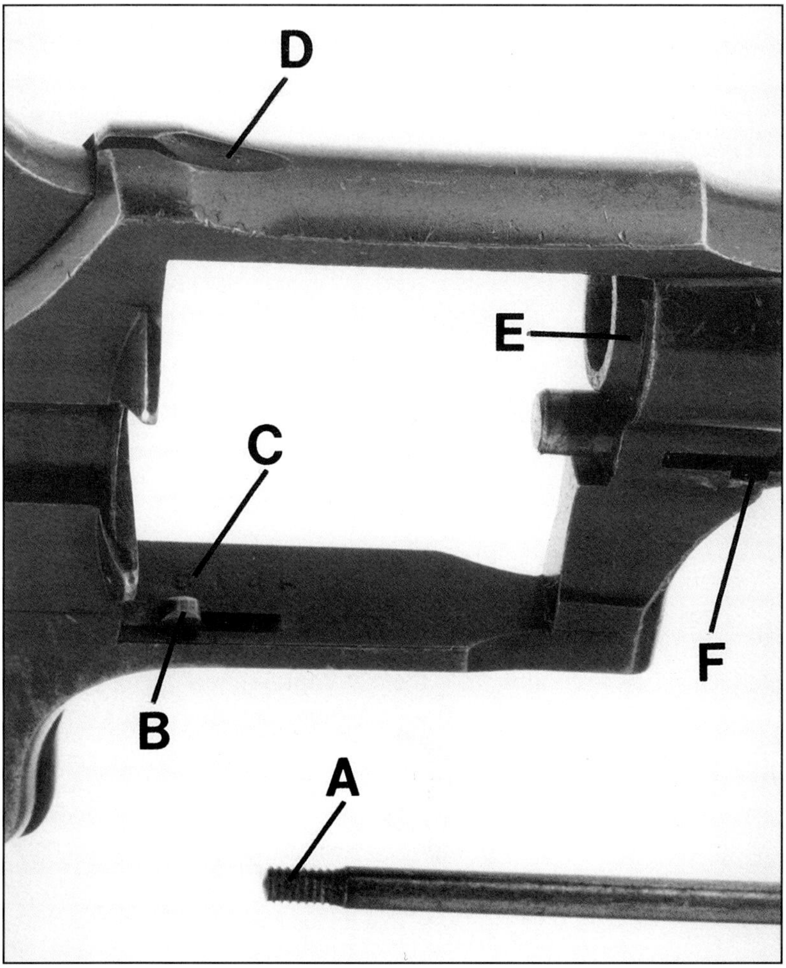

3-02. Detail view of right side of a No. 3 New Model revolver, showing threaded ejector rod (A), cylinder stop (B), serial number (C), arrow-shaped rear sight (D), barrel circumference milling (E), and notch for cylinder base pin latch (F).
R.A. Cooper photograph

Finishes

During this period in firearms history—the early 1870s—small caliber pistols were usually nickel plated, as were the guns referred to as "Saturday Night Specials." It may be assumed that this was an inexpensive finish; however, Remington catalogs of the period show that blue finish actually was slightly cheaper than nickel plate.

Observation of BHO specimens reveals that 70.9% were in nickel plate, while only 11.3% were in blue, and 17.7% were engraved and nickel plated. Examination of Table 3-A and the BHO sample intervals reveals a cluster of finish variations in the intervals "7001" through "11000." Twenty-nine specimens were recorded for all finishes with 6.8% of the sample involved. This variation in finish is enhanced by the recording of five blue specimens, the most for any interval in Table 3-A. In this example 70% of the blue specimens recorded were found in this interval. The interval "13001" to "15000" with twenty-four specimens sampled represents the largest cluster of BHO specimens (38.7%). Returning to the matter of engraved specimens, it was possible to have gilt, *i.e.*, gold-finished parts (hammer, cylinder, trigger, ejector rod), or the entire revolver finished in gold. Some nickel plated pieces have been examined with hammer and/or ejector rod in gold wash. The 1878 catalog refers to engraved revolvers that were "plated and gilt" or the optional "full plate engraved." Apparently the gilt finish was offered in two variations, *i.e.*, gold plate and gold wash, the latter a much duller, non-reflecting finish. Clearly gold wash was the more prevalent variation. Oddly, the catalogs of the period did not discuss the variations or finish distinctions, although one surely could inform Remington of personal finish requirements.

A factory engraved BHO specimen in one collection (photo 3-04) is an excellent example of Remington's factory engraving of the period. When the specimen was compared with another saw handle Remington (photo 3-03, bottom), the engraving was indeed similar in appearance and quality. The BHO engraved specimens examined have had essentially the same motif and appear to have been copied or engraved by the same person or persons (photo 3-03, top). No significant variation in motif, such as that seen in the No. 4 revolver, has been noted.

Types of Grips

The Remington catalogs for 1878 and 1881 offered ivory, pearl, and checkered hard rubber grips. Strangely no reference was made to wood grips, specifically of walnut, which had proved so popular on other Remington revolvers. Even more unusual was the fact that the catalogs did not refer to wood for other models offered for sale. No recorded BHO specimens have been found with Remington factory wood grips. This is viewed as curious, in the light of the number of revolvers observed (see Table 3-A). Some comment should be made here about the "ivory" grips offered to customers and discussed earlier. These grips were a nitrocellulose product known as "celluloid." No dates or documents are available to clarify the use of the "imitation ivory" material. Observation reveals approximately 17.7% with Remington celluloid grips.

In terms of availability, checkered black hard rubber grips were the type most commonly observed on specimens of the No. 3 revolver (approximately

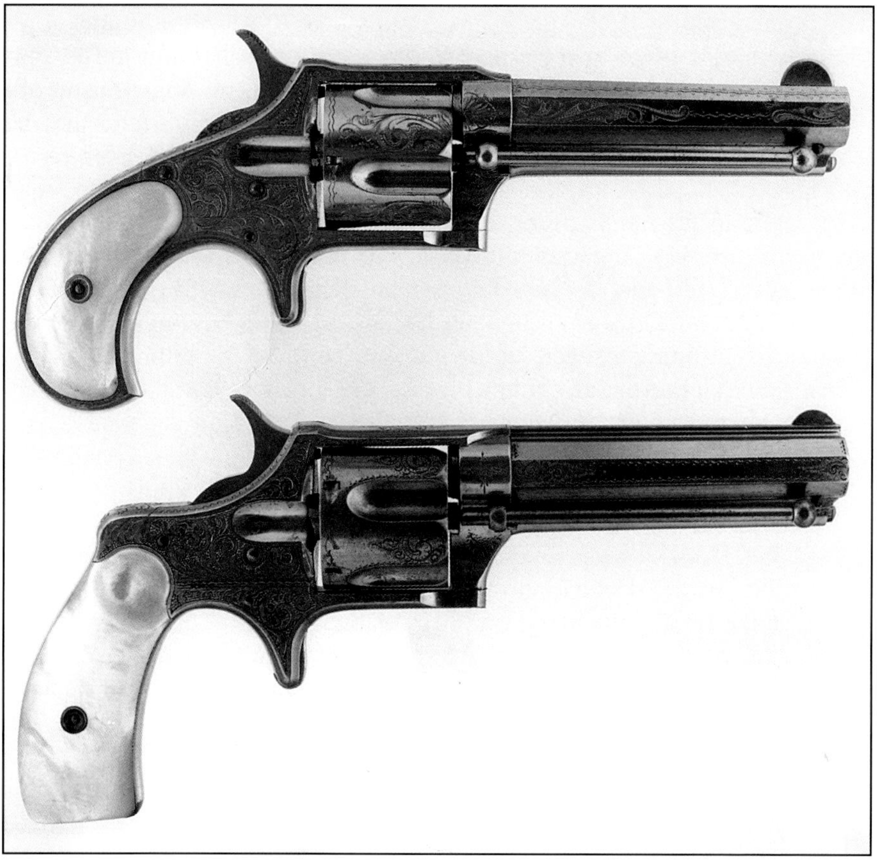

3-03. A pair of Remington No. 3 New Model revolvers factory engraved in the pattern typical for the model, nickel plated, mother-of-pearl grips, showing variations in grip style. Bird-head grip (top) serial number "7789," .38 rimfire caliber; saw handle grip (bottom) serial number "27859," also .38 rimfire caliber. *R.A. Cooper photograph*

74.2%). However, rubber grips were not advertised as an option. Occasionally smooth black hard rubber grips have been observed, but only a few were recorded. Some specimens have been examined with grips of dark brown hard rubber, although always in a checkered style.

Mother of pearl grips were available, and would logically be expected to accompany an engraved revolver. Several engraved specimens have been examined with original hard rubber grips (photo 3-04). Records reveal approximately 6.4% of the revolver sample were sold with pearl grips. One explanation for so few pearl-gripped revolvers may have been that Remington catalogs of the period indicated the cost of pearl at 20% more than "ivory." Black hard rubber grips were obviously what Remington provided for a basic order.

Hammer

Remington case-hardened the hammer and trigger components of its arms. With the BHO, these parts were often finished in nickel plate, blue, or gilt to match or complement the balance of the piece. Some production models were sold with only the case-hardened finish exposed. All hammer spurs had a knurled or cross-hatched surface.

Trigger

All trigger surfaces were made in a smooth finish. Since the trigger housing exposes little more than the trigger surface, no engraving was possible. No specimens have been examined having any variations.

Springs

Interior springs appear quite durable, and remarkably few specimens seen showed any weakness or loss of tension. The limited number of springs involved in the revolver's operation provides one of the reasons for the survival rate. The high quality of steel is an additional reason for the presence of so many intact specimens. The ejector rod spring on the No. 1 and No. 2 models had been noted as being less durable and readily affected by hard use.

3-04. A factory engraved No. 3 New Model revolver, serial number "13531," nickel plated with hard rubber grips. Caliber .38 centerfire. Octagonal barrel, bird-head grips; note large front sight. *Ex: Karl F. Moldenhauer collection; H. Poisson photograph*

Screws

All Remington revolver screws are soft and easily misshaped by the use of improperly sized screwdrivers. Those of the BHO were no exception. Because they were not case-hardened, they were easily ruptured in removal if care was not taken. All revolver screws were blued regardless of the finish on the balance of the piece.

Markings

Serial number marking was discussed earlier, and, while important, it is not one of the distinguishing features of this firearm. The most prominent marking appears on the barrel. All production revolvers were stamped "E. Remington & Sons, Ilion, N.Y., Pat. W.S. Smoot, Oct. 21, 1873," reading from muzzle to breech all on one line. No variations in type font have been noted.

The cylinder was not uniformly marked or numbered, nor were the trigger, hammer, cylinder center pin, or other internal parts. No other markings distinguish the production revolver. Occasional specimens have been noted having irregularly stamped numbers and some few have shown a mixed numerals font.

Sights

Front sights were made in two sizes ($^{5}/_{16}$ inch by $^{1}/_{8}$ inch, and ½ inch by ¼ inch). Both were finished in nickel plate and uniformly recessed into the barrel flat $^{1}/_{8}$ inch from the muzzle. The 1878 and 1881 Remington catalogs show the small sights on the model pictured, while Karr and Karr showed the model with the large sight.[4] Photo 3-01 shows the two sight variations on specimens in a collection. The rear sight is an arrow-like notch milled into the top of the frame (photo 3-02).

The incidence of the large front sight on BHO revolvers was more prevalent than the small, accounting for 62.2% recorded. Analysis of the BHO sample reveals that an interesting serial number clustering occurred in two intervals—"7001" to "11000," and "13001" to "15000." From serial number "8055" to "9266" the small sight was found in 37.8%. Nowhere else in the intervals (see Table 3-A) were any BHO small front sights recorded. Once again, no mention is made in the catalogs regarding the availability of front sights in two sizes. While a knowledgeable customer likely could specify his choice, the lack of discussion on the relative merits of each size does not portray aggressive product marketing by Remington.

Barrel and Frame Assembly

As noted earlier, the BHO was made with an octagon-shaped barrel that was machined separately and then threaded into the frame. Careful observation of a specimen reveals a web-like addition, or channel, below the barrel designed to house the cylinder center pin, ejector rod, and spring (photo 3-05.) This web-like element was machined integral with the barrel, from a single piece of steel. The forerunner for such a barrel configuration and ejector housing has been found in the Smoot's Patent No. 1 and No. 2 revolvers.

All revolvers recorded have had a uniform barrel length of 3¾ inches,

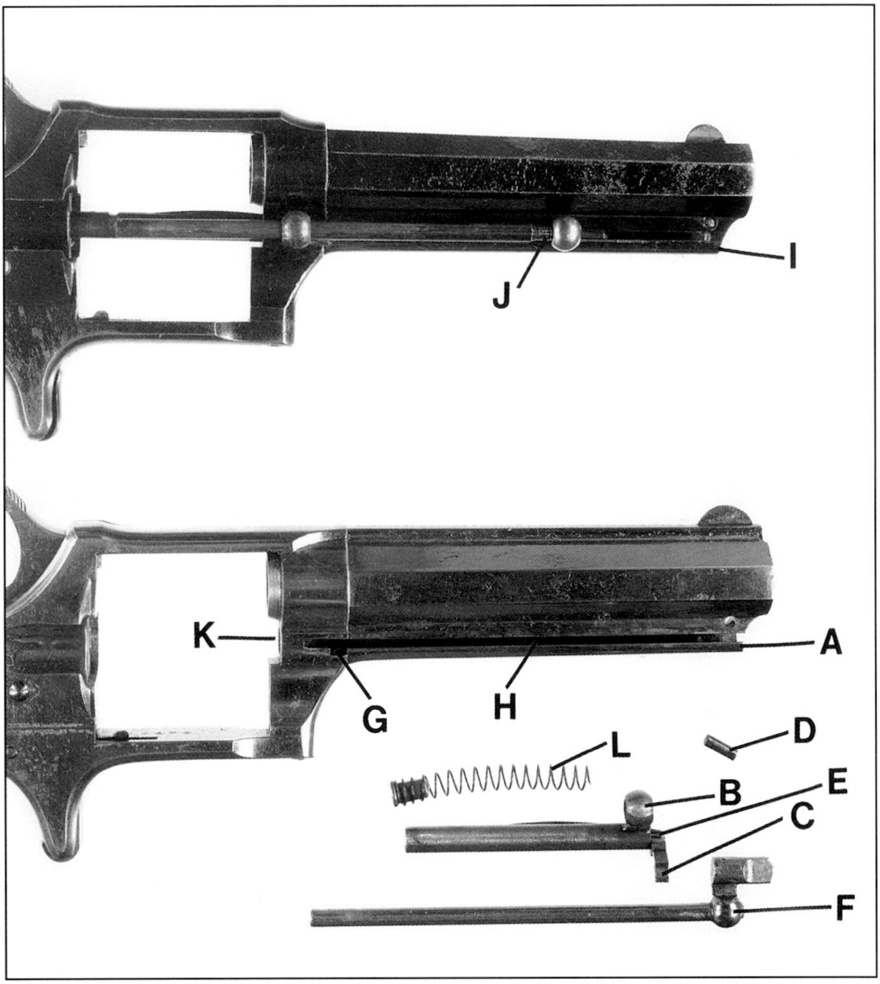

3-05. Detail view of two disassembled No. 3 New Model revolvers, showing (top) closed ejector channel under muzzle (I), partially threaded ejector rod (J) which slides in round guide on the cylinder base pin (B). Bottom gun shows the open slot at front of ejector web (A), ejector channel under barrel (H), notch (G) for cylinder base pin latch (C), ejector spring (L), retaining pin (D), ejector rod (F), cylinder pin spring (E), and milling (K). *R.A. Cooper photograph*

with no specimen observed showing any variation. That raises the question of why specimens did not appear with slightly longer barrels, considering the caliber and size of the No. 3 revolver. All barrels have five-groove rifling.

Cylinder Center Pin and Shell Ejection System

The BHO cylinder center pin is similar to that of the Smoot's Patent No. 1 and No. 2 revolvers, except that the ejector rod fits through a spherical-shaped lug on the end of the cylinder center pin. This spherical lug has a knurled surface on both top and bottom to aid in grasping it securely (photo 3-05). Alongside the spherical lug, on the center pin, is a spring-held latch pin. This spring also extends into the cylinder pin shaft in which it is recessed (photo 3-05). This latch pin catch normally fits into a notch cut into the slot machined into the channel below the barrel (photos 3-02 and 3-05). In order to slide the cylinder pin toward the muzzle, this catch must be freed from the notch by lifting it upward against the ejector rod. The spring-held catch has enough tension to remain in the notch unless lifted. This notch was a critical feature, for it prevents the cylinder center pin from sliding forward and releasing the cylinder while in use.

The cylinder center pin is $1^{15}/_{16}$ inches long, and all specimens examined to date appeared case-hardened and nickel plated. A small arched spring recessed into the pin shaft, which also extends to the latch pin-catch, was meant to control the revolutions or freedom of the cylinder (photo 3-05). These springs are reasonably sturdy, although ease of firing was affected when they became damaged or bent. Any change in the angle of the cylinder center pin or alignment of its spherical lug affects the ease of removal from the cylinder itself, as

Remington No. 3 Revolver.

NEW MODEL.

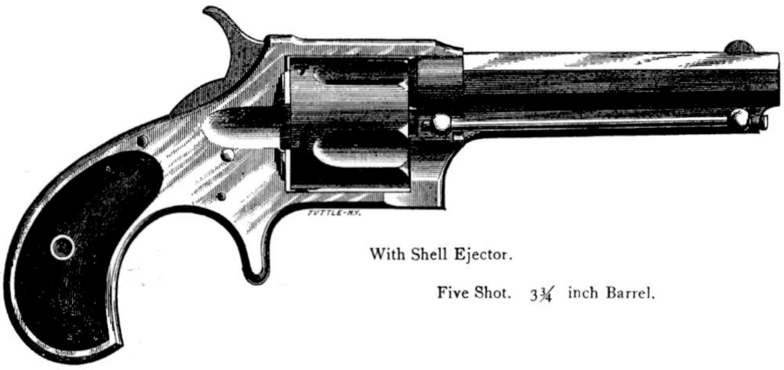

38 Calibre, Rim or Center Fire. Designed especially for House or Belt Pistol. The center fire shells can be reloaded thus reducing the cost of ammunition.

Length of Pistol 7¾ in. Weight 15 oz. Finished in best manner, with forged Steel Frame and Checkered Rubber Stocks.

well as from the channel in which the cylinder center pin is housed. The shell ejection system, like the preceding Smoot's Patent models No. 1 and No. 2, allows the spring-fed ejector rod to push the shells out of the cylinder by simply lining up the chamber openings. The ejector rod itself is 3¼ inches long and threaded into the spherical lug at the muzzle end of the ejector rod (photos 3-02 and 3-05). The spherical lug is identical to the one connected to the cylinder center pin and is machined into a cylindrical-shaped piece of metal that fits through the slot and into the web-like channel below the barrel (photo 3-05). The small cylinder center pin, ejector spring, and spherical lug at the muzzle end cannot be removed because of the web metal below the pin (photo 3-05). This milling fault was corrected in the SH variation, so that all of these parts could be removed from the channel for cleaning and/or replacement (photo 3-05). Within this channel is a spring designed to offer sufficient tension to eject shells and to prevent the ejector rod from sliding freely. This tension requires that the ejector rod be retained against the muzzle end of the channel to prevent it from sliding into the cylinder during operation of the revolver. These springs, although reasonably adequate, were subject to wear, and careless use easily affected the revolver's performance. Any reduction in either the size or length of the spring clearly affects the operation of the shell-ejecting system.

Many specimens have been examined with damaged cylinder center pins, bent spherical lugs, missing latch pin catches, bent ejector rods, and dented channel slots, yet the cylinder center pin and shell ejection system are nevertheless an effective and skillfully designed feature of this model.

Bushings

All cylinders have a short bushing ($^{3}/_{32}$ inch) in front of the cylinder and a ratchet bushing ($^{1}/_{8}$ inch) in the rear, which engages a hand or pawl attached to the hammer assembly. Both bushing and ratchet were essentially uniform on the BHO, although some specimens have been observed with minor variations in size.

Cylinders

All standard production model cylinders measure $1^{3}/_{16}$ inches long, have five flutes, and are related to a five-shot revolver. No specimen has been examined without the cylinder flutes; neither has a specimen been recorded in any caliber other than .38.

Cylinder notches (photo 3-06) to lock the cylinder in line with the barrel are uniform, and no specimens have been examined having any variations. The cylinder notches are engaged by a cylinder stop connected to the trigger housing (photo 3-02), and have been observed as being reasonably sturdy and reliable. This stop was coordinated with the hammer assembly, and drops into the floor plate above the trigger to allow the cylinder to rotate. A spring above the

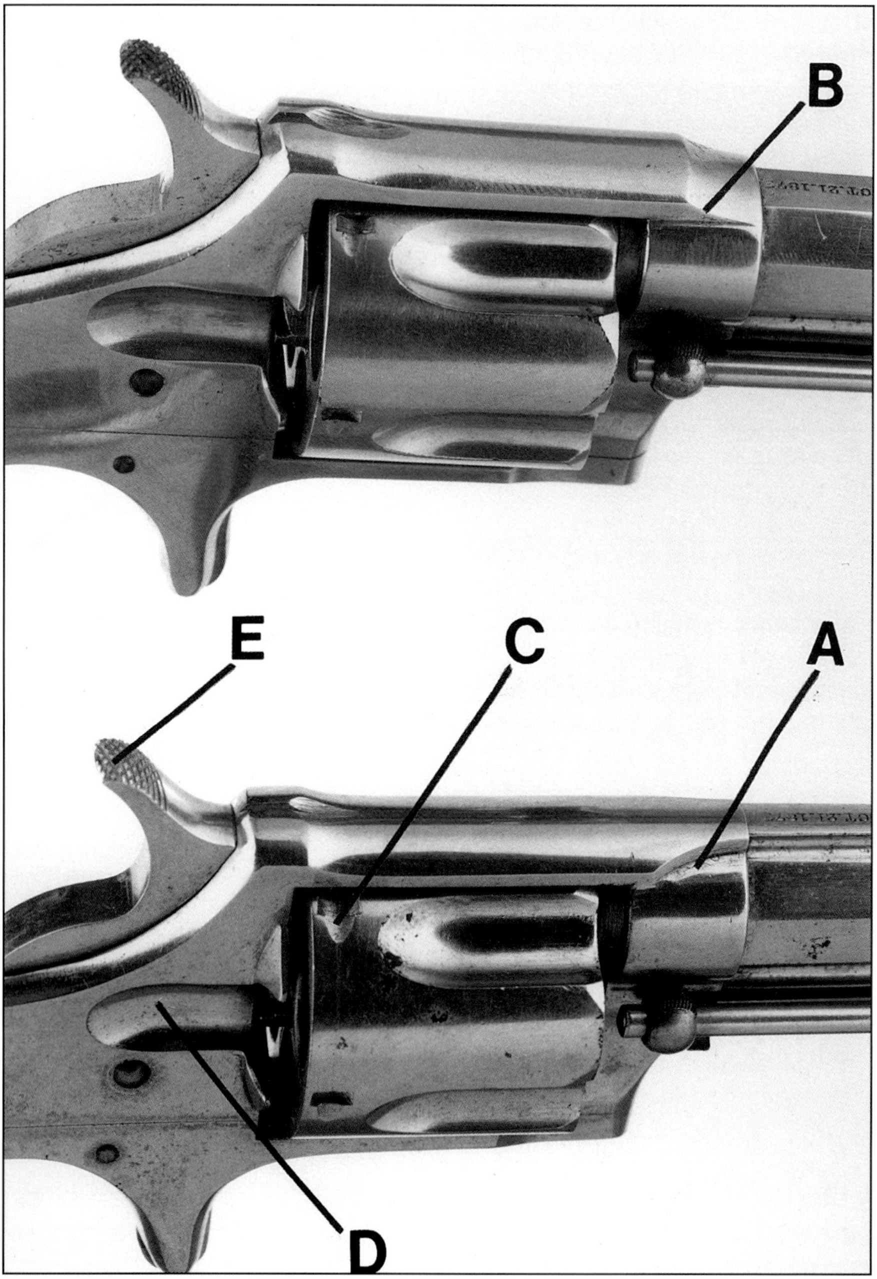

3-06. Detail view of two disassembled No. 3 New Model revolvers, showing milling of top strap at barrel-frame juncture of BHO model (B) and SH model (A), hammer knurling (E), shell ejector flute (D), and cylinder stops (C). *R.A. Cooper photograph*

trigger places tension on the stop in an upward direction in order to engage each notch as the cylinder rotates. Thus, when the hammer is placed on full cock, the stop in the floor plate drops into a recessed slot until one-fifth of a turn is completed, then rises up to engage the cylinder notch.

Milling

A single type of frame milling has been noted for the BHO, specifically where the barrel is exposed as it joins the frame in front of the cylinder. Clearly evident is the exposure of a circular dimension to the barrel extension and a cutaway from the frame to below the front cylinder bushing (photos 3-02 and 3-05). This width before the cylinder and frame is approximately $^{3}/_{32}$ inch and is essentially uniform on all No. 3 revolvers.

Recoil Shield

All BHO revolvers have a uniform size and shape to the recoil shield. On the left side it is arc-like, following the outer lines of the cylinder, while the right side is for loading, with a ½ inch wide opening for shell insertion. An $^{11}/_{16}$ inch long by $^{11}/_{32}$ inch wide flute on the right frame is standard on all BHO revolvers, to aid in the ease of cartridge insertion and removal (photos 3-01 and 3-06).

Summary

The Remington Smoot's Patent No. 3 BHO revolver had serial numbering identified up to serial "15513." Significant gaps in sampling, along with no specimens in one interval, prevent a conclusion that production of approximately 15,000 revolvers occurred. A more credible estimate might be 12,000.

No. 3 Bird-Head, Top-Ribbed Barrel (BHR) Revolver

As noted, the format of this chapter provides a separate category for discussing the top-ribbed barrel variation (BHR). None of the Remington catalogs from the period, nor the picture in the Karr and Karr book[5], describe it. Somers did not discuss this variation in his article.[6] One alert collector identified the distinction in a letter to the editor.[7]

The importance of this ribbed barrel is that it later became a distinguishing feature of the No. 3 saw handle (SH) variation (photo 3-07). The BHR followed the BHO in production, and was offered for sale in the 1882 catalog. Since the barrel variation was clearly a transitional feature, some evidence of its serial number articulation with the saw handle variation confirms this production change. No photo cut of the BHR was shown in Remington catalogs after 1882.

3-07. A pair of Remington No. 3 New Model revolvers, showing bird-head grip, top ribbed barrel, nickel plating (top), and saw handle grip, blued finish (bottom). Note differences in hard rubber grip styles. *R.A. Cooper photograph*

Serial Number Data

The bird-head, top-ribbed specimens were evident in two serial number intervals: "15500" through "17000," and "17001" through "19000," with forty-one specimens accounting for 79.9% of the sample. The other two intervals showed single-digit frequency, or 24.1% (see Table 3-B). The presence of the majority of the sample early in the serial numbering suggests that production changes were being considered. Gaps in serial numbered specimens within any interval amounted to no more than several hundred digits. This limitation in sampling relates to a smaller production availability. This sampling limitation has been noted over the years where incidence was clearly less than the BHO variation.

Statistical Treatment

Based on observed serial numbers from "15513" to "22111," the statistical estimate is 6,898 revolvers manufactured, with a 95% confidence factor.

Serial Number Location and Stamping Practice

In the No. 3 BHR variation serial number stamping is found on the top and bottom straps of the cylinder area. The cylinder must be removed in order to read the No. 3 serial number; or the frame can be dismounted and the same end achieved. This BHR variation has no serial numbering in any other location.

Caliber Data

Of unusual significance in caliber information is that all specimens in the sample were in .38 rimfire. By comparison, only 54.8% of the BHO recorded were .38 rimfire. Even though Remington advertised the reloading of centerfire shells as an economic issue, and publicly reported the incidence of rimfire cartridge misfire, neither issue reduced the incidence of rimfire caliber preference. It is certainly not reflected in the accumulation of data.

Finishes

With regard to finish, the BHR serial number intervals (see Table 3-B) were quite distinct when compared to the BHO. Fifty-one specimens (94.4%) in the sample were recorded with nickel finish. Only one specimen was recorded for revolvers having blue finish. The frequency distribution for nickel plated examples follows the observed frequency in the intervals. In a sampling of fifty-one specimens, to find only three with a finish other than nickel plate seems unique in light of the distribution found in other models and variations.

Types of Grips

Table 3-B illustrates the distribution of grip materials for the BHR sample. Checkered hard rubber has been identified for 81.5% of the sample. Generally, hard rubber grips were black in color, although a dark brown has been seen. Remington "ivory" (celluloid) grips were found on 7.4% of the specimens. Only one specimen each was recorded as having pearl or walnut grips. Three specimens were identified with unknown material. When the grip material for the BHR was compared with the BHO, the percentages for each grip material were similar. The occurrence of checkered hard rubber is closely comparable for both variations. Remington celluloid is more obvious on the BHO variation, accounting for 17.7% versus 7.4% for the BHR. Pearl was also more evident for the BHO than the BHR. More BHR than BHO specimens have different grip materials.

Table 3-B

No. 3 bird-head top rib barrel sample frequency for caliber, finish and grip material for all serial number intervals.

		Caliber		Finish			
Serial No. Intervals	Frequency	Rimfire	Centerfire	Nickel	Blue	Engraved	Mixed
15,500 - 17,000	22	22		21			1
17,001 - 19,000	19	19		19			
19,001 - 21,000	5	5		4		1	
21,001 - 23,000	8	8		7	1		
TOTAL	54	54		51	1	1	1
Percentage		100%		94.4%	1.8%	1.8%	1.8%

	Grip Material						
Serial No. Intervals	1 Walnut	2 Rose.	3 Pearl	4 Cell.	5 Ivory	6 Chkr. Rubber	7 Unknown
15,500 - 17,000	1			1		18	2
17,001 - 19,000				1	1	17	
19,001 - 21,000				1		4	
21,001 - 23,000			1	1		5	1
TOTAL	1		1	4	1	44	3
Percentage	1.8%		1.8%	7.4%	1.8%	81.5%	5.5%

1. Walnut 2. Rosewood 3. Pearl 4. Celluloid 5. Ivory 6. Checkered Rubber 7. Unknown

*Not included in this table: Gold and mixed-finish specimens.

Hammer, Trigger, Springs, Screws, and Markings

Production features discussed earlier for these elements in the BHO are essentially identical for the BHR.

Sights

A small front sight $^{13}/_{32}$ inch in length at the base by $^{1}/_{8}$ inch high is recessed into the rib flat. This represents the standard sight, which is uniformly nickel plated.

Barrel and Frame Assembly

The barrel, with its top rib, was made of a single piece of steel. The rib measures $^{3}/_{32}$ inch high by $^{5}/_{32}$ inch wide at the flat above the barrel's basic octagon shape. No variations in these dimensions have been noted.

Cylinder Center Pin and Shell Ejection System

As discussed earlier, for the BHO the ejector spring channel slot is closed below the muzzle (upper versus lower example, photo 3-05). This feature prevents removal of the cylinder center pin and ejector spring and rod (photo 3-05). On the BHR, this small piece of metal was removed and only a small drift pin substituted to retain all parts in the channel (photo 3-05). Removing this pin is not easy compared to a screw, as it can only be removed with a proper size punch.

Bushings, Cylinders, Milling, and Recoil Shield

These BHR revolver features, with the exception of milling, are essentially identical to those of the BHO. Milling of the BHR, particularly where the top of the frame joins the barrel, is smoothly curved. This differs from the BHO, which has straight front-to-back lines on the top of the frame (photo 3-06, parts A and B). The barrel appears to be the only distinguishing change; all other aspects of the BHR are identical to those of the BHO. Moreover, internal parts are interchangeable.

Summary

The BHR is essentially a ribbed barrel variation made exclusively in .38 rimfire caliber. Over 90% are finished in nickel plate. Only one specimen each has been recorded for blue, engraved, or mixed finishes. The BHO sample was 13% larger than the BHR, and the ribbed barrel model is seen less frequently and found in fewer collections. However, it is estimated that Remington manufactured at least 12,000 and perhaps more than 15,600 BHR revolvers.

Remington No. 3, New Model, Saw Handle Grip (SH) Revolver

Remington first announced the availability of this "New Model" in its June, 1882 catalog. It also provided a photo cut to inform the customer that this revolver was different from the BHO. Curiously, no catalog photo cut was ever provided for the BHR. The saw handle (SH)-gripped version was, therefore, new and different (photo 3-03). As noted earlier, the top ribbed barrel feature of the BHR became the barrel shape for the saw handle variation. All other aspects of the frame parting design, external/internal parts, and the basic assembly of the BHR were retained, except for the grip frame for the SH. No information is available as to why Remington chose to use the saw handle-shaped grip frame in place of the earlier bird-head shape. This was clearly a grip configuration change away from that of any other revolver Remington had manufactured from the 1870s through the early 1880s.

Serial Number Data

As noted earlier, serial numbering on some Remington models continued in service from an older to a new model or variation. With the No. 3 BHO Smoot's Patent revolver, numbering began in the BHO and continued through the saw handle variation with five-digit serial numbers.

The lowest serial number recorded for the SH was "23244," and the highest "27881." Table 3-C presents the sample frequency in the five intervals. All intervals have specimens that are nearly comparable, with the exception of "27001," which has over twice the frequency of the other intervals.

In over four decades of examining and recording data on SH specimens, it became evident that many did not have serial numbers. Over time it was concluded that approximately half the specimens examined bore no serial numbers. More specifically, among the models discussed in this volume, only the SH variation exhibited this trait. The logical conclusion about this phenomenon is that Remington simply manufactured and sold these revolvers without serial numbers. Apparently, during this period in Remington's manufacturing history the use of serial numbers was a means of identification solely for the manufacturer's convenience. Since it was not essential to a sale, it need not have been provided.

The lack of serial numbers on an estimated 50% of examined SH specimens cannot be attributed to worker theft, production flaws, or worker indifference; rather, it seems the likely result of some company policy. In the absence of known or written company purpose, no other reason can be postulated save minimal production time.

Table 3-C

No. 3 saw handle octagon barrel sample frequency for caliber, finish and grip material for all serial number intervals.

		Caliber		Finish			
Serial No. Intervals	Frequency	Rimfire	Centerfire	Nickel	Blue	Engraved	Mixed
23,001 - 24,000	13	12	1	8		4	1
24,001 - 25,000	15	15		14		1	
25,001 - 26,000	11	10	1	11			
26,001 - 27,000	12	11	1	9		3	
27,001 - 28,000	31	15	16	23	2	6	
TOTAL	82	63	19	65	2	14	1
Percentage		76.8%	23.2%	79.3%	2.4%	17.1%	1.2%

Grip Material							
Serial No. Intervals	1 Walnut	2 Rose.	3 Pearl	4 Cell.	5 Ivory	6 Chkr. Rubber	7 Unknown
23,001 - 24,000			4	1		8	
24,001 - 25,000			2			11	2
25,001 - 26,000			1			8	2
26,001 - 27,000		1	2			9	
27,001 - 28,000	3		8	2		18	
TOTAL	3	1	17	3		54	4
Percentage	3.6%	1.2%	20.7%	3.6%		65.8%	4.9%

1. Walnut 2. Rosewood 3. Pearl 4. Celluloid 5. Ivory 6. Checkered Rubber 7. Unknown

*Not included in this table: Gold and mixed-finish specimens.

Estimates of No. 3 Saw Handle Production

Despite the fact that every other SH examined had no serial numbers, some production estimate must be made. Our calculation is as follows: The lowest serial number recorded was "23244," and the highest was "27881," which implies a maximum production of 5,000 specimens.

Statistical Treatment

The eighty-two specimens examined generated a statistical estimate of 4,810 SH revolvers produced, at most. However, if the unnumbered specimens followed those with serial numbers, then it is possible that as many as 9,600 were made.

Serial Number Location and Stamping Practice

Similar to the practice with the BHO and BHR, the serial number placement on SH revolvers is on the top and bottom strap enclosing the cylinder area. With the SH, serial numbers were not placed in any other location. One exception (number "27837") has been recorded by Moldenhauer[8], in which the serial number was stamped on the butt as well as in the usual places. The use of single digits, which appear on the grip frame or elsewhere, is interpreted as some type of assembly coding.

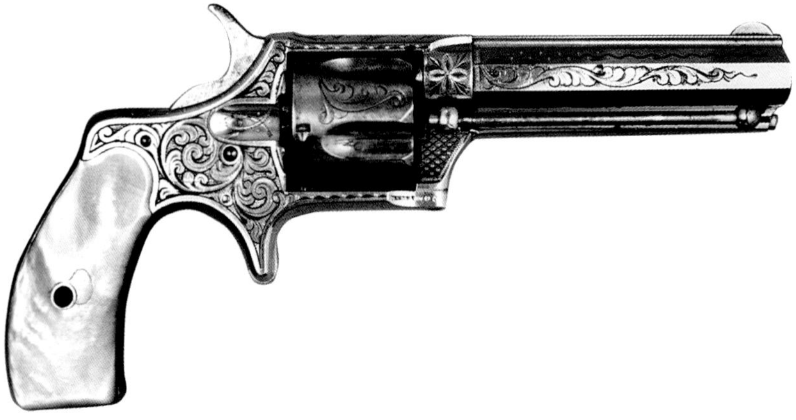

3-08. Remington No. 3 New Model revolver with saw handle grip, serial number "23578." Factory engraved, nickel plated, gold washed cylinder and hammer, mother-of-pearl grips. Caliber .38 rimfire. *Ex: Fritz Baehr collection and photograph*

3-09. A Remington No. 3 New Model revolver, factory engraved in a pattern more ornate than usually seen on the saw handle variation. Serial number "27409," caliber .38 rimfire. *Ex: Karl F. Moldenhauer collection; H. Poisson photograph*

Caliber Data

The 1882 Remington catalog indicated that the SH was available in .38 rimfire and centerfire calibers. The catalog also indicated that centerfire shells could be reloaded, thus reducing the cost of ammunition.

Table 3-C describes the distribution by serial number intervals. All intervals had nearly comparable frequencies, except interval "27001" to "28000," which at thirty-one was over twice that of the other intervals. This interval represents 37.8% of all the sample specimens. The obvious caliber in the sample was .38 rimfire, which dominated with 76.8%. Only a single specimen was recorded for centerfire in all other intervals except "27001." In this interval, sixteen specimens in centerfire amounted to 84% of all centerfire revolvers recorded. This suggests that centerfire apparently enjoyed a resurgence in popularity in the mid-to-late 1880s. However, rimfire for the SH represented three out of four sales in this sample. This suggests that it may have taken some time before the savings of reloading centerfire cartridges appealed to customers.

Finishes

This period in firearms history seemed to favor the nickel plate finish. Remington SH revolvers tend to follow the trend, with sixty-five (79.3%) specimens recorded in this finish. Fourteen engraved specimens represent 17.1% of the sample (photos 3-08 and 3-09), while two blue specimens account for 2.4% (photo 3-07). While blue finish is nearly absent from the SH sample, it was cheaper than nickel, as noted in the 1882 Remington catalog. As has been the case with other Remington revolvers, gold or gilt finish was advertised and the customer could request the part or parts to be so finished. Photo 3-03 illustrates a factory engraved specimen with the usual motif and quality. Photo 3-08 shows another standard, *i.e.*, factory engraved specimen. A slightly more ornate pattern, the work of a different engraver, is pictured in photo 3-09.

Types of Grips

The 1882 catalog indicated that checkered hard rubber "stocks" were standard, with pearl and ivory also available. The sample revealed that fifty-four specimens (65.8%) had checkered hard rubber, seventeen specimens (20.7%) had pearl, three (3.6%) had walnut, and three (3.6%) had Remington celluloid grips. One specimen's grips were of rosewood, while four had non-factory wood replacements. Compared to the BHR, the six grip materials recorded for the SH are similar. Checkered hard rubber (65.8%) and pearl (20.7%) grips dominated the types recorded. When compared with the BHR, the SH had a somewhat greater incidence of other grip materials.

The saw handle-shaped hard rubber grips were also checkered, and featured an encircled, old English-style "R" or medallion at the top (photo 3-07). A diamond design surrounds the grip screw, plus a *fleur-de-lis* like design beneath the initial and at the base. Both black and dark brown colors have been recorded. Although three specimens in the sample were recorded in Remington celluloid, no SH specimen has been found with genuine ivory grips. Although the 1882 catalog made no mention that wood grips could be ordered, one specimen marked "U.S. Express Company" has factory-quality walnut grips.[9] Another specimen (serial number "27871") has walnut grips, but they are stamped with the number "27848." It cannot be determined if these grips were originally shipped with this specimen. Certainly the presence of a different number on the grips with credible digits complicates the matter of establishing the history of the specimen.

Table 3-C identifies the interval for the serial number of the specimen and the grips. The close proximity of the digits for the specimen and for the grips identifies the grip number as at least belonging to the production period.

Hammer, Trigger, Springs, and Screws

All of the discussion regarding these elements for the BHO and BHR revolvers apply to the SH. All parts are interchangeable in each of the three variations.

Markings

The barrel markings on all production SH revolvers are identical to those of the BHO and BHR revolvers. No variations in type font have been noted for the SH, and none of the interior parts are uniformly marked or numbered.

Sights

The front sight on SH revolvers is identical to that of the BHR. Likewise, for the rear sight an arrow-like notch is milled into the top of the frame as found on the BHR. No production variation has been noted.

Barrel and Frame Assembly

As discussed earlier, the BHR variation features the distinctive top rib on its barrel. This, then, became the singular barrel style for the SH. No barrel length variations have been noted. All production barrels have five-groove rifling.

Cylinder Center Pin and Shell Ejection System

The SH variation is equipped with the same cylinder center pin and shell ejection system found in the BHO and BHR revolvers. The only minor variation noted is in the ejector rod that was not threaded into the spherical lug at the muzzle end of the webbed channel (photo 3-05, part F). No production variations have been identified for this element.

Bushings, Cylinder, Milling, and Recoil Shield

All data discussed for the BHO and the BHR on these key component parts apply to the SH. Dimension similarity and interchangeability of the cylinder among the three variations of Remington's No. 3 revolvers was retained.

Summary

The SH was available in both .38 rimfire and centerfire calibers, in all available finishes as well as in all grip materials. Its distinctive grip frame is unique among Remington revolver shapes. Certainly it is distinct when compared with the bird-head grip shape of the BHO and BHR. Moreover, all three No. 3 revolver variations have interchangeable parts. A production estimate of 9600 pieces was arrived at by taking into account that as many were observed with as without serial numbers. The SH is the only variation for which this is true.

The production variations described, the distinct manufacturing changes, and the categorical evidence make the No. 3 revolver actually three different firearms. Each is sufficiently separate as to have its own identity, and each is deserving of being called a "New Model." Observation of these three variations suggests that approximately 27,000 were produced, possibly as many as 32,000.

That Remington had financing, corporate restructuring, and business management problems was generally understood within the company, as has been explained. The matter of sales policy and marketing, especially for the No. 3 New Model revolver variations, was not understood. Remington failed to promote their availability, specifically for the No. 3 New Model revolver, through the company's catalogs and price lists, which were the only media of sales advertisement. However, the existing revolvers make irrefutable their individual merit as firearms. These revolvers sustain the lasting reputation of Remington as a distinguished contributor to the history of American firearms manufacturing.

Notes:

1. Charles L. Karr, Jr. and Carroll R. Karr, *Remington Handguns* (2nd edition), 1951, p. 121.
2. *Ibid.*, pp. 121, 123.
3. *Ibid.*, p. 121.
4. *Ibid.*, p. 120.
5. *Ibid.*, p. 121.
6. James R. Somers, "The Remington New Line Revolvers," in *The Texas Gun Collector*, Vol. 59, June 1955, p. 34.
7. _____, Letter to the Editor, in *The Texas Gun Collector*, Vol. 64, November 1955, p. 35.
8. *Public Auction of the Karl F. Moldenhauer Collection of Remington Arms*, 1980, p. 254.
9. *Ibid.*, p. 254.

REMINGTON No. 4 REVOLVER.

NEW MODEL.

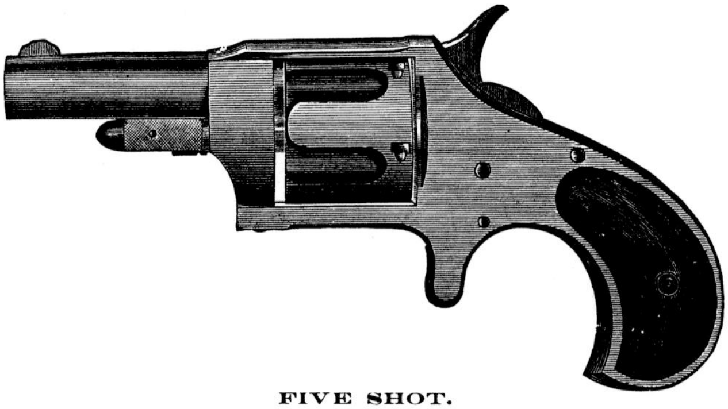

FIVE SHOT.

Length of Pistol 6½ inches. Weight 13 oz. .38 and .41 Calibre. Finished in best manner, with forged Steel Frame and Checkered Rubber Stock.

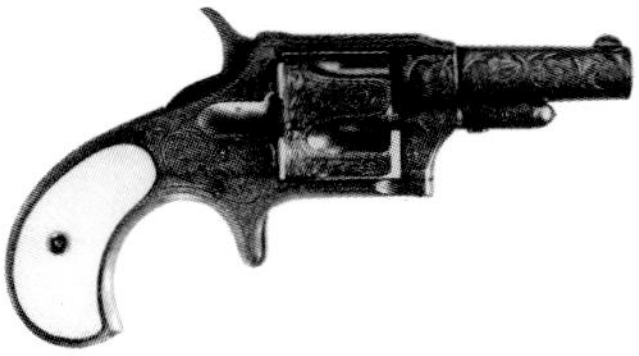

Chapter IV

Remington No. 4 New Model Revolver

The name of the revolver in this chapter may not be familiar to many gun collectors, hence the need to refer to the accompanying photographs. It was frequently called the "New Line No. 4," and even a "Smoot." A specimen of this Remington revolver can be found at nearly every gun show in the United States. But although this model has been available for many years, collector literature has revealed only two articles devoted exclusively to this firearm.[1] With reference to its name, none of the catalogs of the period referred to it as a "New Line." In 1877 the Remington catalog announced the availability of the No. 4 for the first time and featured a photo cut to illustrate it. Remington catalogs showed the No. 4 for sale through 1884; from 1885 through 1887 the names Lamberson, Furman & Company (New York) and D.H. Lawrence (Chicago) were listed on the catalog covers as Remington's sole agents. Both advertised the No. 4 model for sale. It can be assumed that production of the No. 4 ceased with the receivership and sale of Remington in 1888.

Typically, company catalogs pictured the No. 4 revolver along with the three Smoot's Patent models. Grouping these four models together may have been by design, because of an assigned number to each. While there are some frame assembly similarities between the No. 4 and the three Smoot's Patent models, the No. 4 was given no patent designation. Remington used the term "New Model" for the No. 4 as well as for the other models. The No. 4 does have important differences from the Smoot's Patent revolvers. Specifically they are in cylinder base pin operation, a separate round barrel fabrication, cartridge ejector, and frame-milling variations.

Serial Number Data

One might expect that logic would call for numbering a new model beginning with serial number "1," and continuing until production was terminated. However, other Remington researchers have indicated that occasionally serial numbers on certain models were continued without interruption to the next, or companion, model. Such was the case with the three Smoot's Patent models.

Numbering for the No. 4 revolver sample shows the existence of serial number "2" (see Table 4-A). The highest number recorded was serial number

"23039." The records of serial numbers show that for this range of numbers, gaps or breaks between any series were no larger than approximately 1,000, with the exception of serial numbers "15549" to "18108." Within each series of 1,000, recorded specimens indicate serial numbers of approximately two revolvers sampled for each 100 numbers. Thus, it may be inferred that with additional observed specimens, these serial number gaps would close.

Estimate of No. 4 Production

It can be concluded that Remington probably produced the quantity of No. 4 revolvers suggested by the upper limit of the serial number range.

Statistical Treatment

Using the formula proposed in this volume, a statistical estimate of 23,314 was obtained with a 95% confidence factor. That number is double what Karr and Karr indicated[2] (see Table 4-A).

While Remington used repetitive or "batch" numbering with its other models, there is no evidence that duplicate numbering was used with the No. 4 revolver. When serial number data ranges are reviewed, a pattern appears with reference to caliber designation and finish.

Given the adequate total number sample, the lack of specimen incidence in serial number interval "16001" to "18000" suggests that Remington may have made a deliberate decision toward terminating production. This hypothesis is supported by the presence of single-digit frequency within interval "14001" to "16000." Interestingly, in this interval all nine specimens were .41 centerfire caliber. Apparently, .41 caliber was less popular than .38 caliber, since no .41 caliber specimens were observed after this interval. The drop-off in specimens may have been related to a proposed reduction or termination in production of the No. 4 revolver.

Over the No. 4 revolver's decade of production, there appears to be some evidence that serial numbers were assigned or grouped according to caliber and/or finish. Caliber variations required milling the frames to use rimfire or centerfire cartridges, a hammer firing pin milled for either, and cylinder boring. This meant that the No. 4 revolver could not be stored for future sale. Finish was clearly the last step following the milling and boring processes. Completion of an order required the selection of grips, for which six out of ten were hard rubber. Looking at Table 4-A, revolvers in .38 or .41 rimfire caliber finished in nickel could have been produced ahead of time and stored. The only caliber not observed in the intervals after serial number "14000" was .41 rimfire. Since no .38 rimfire specimens were found in intervals "14001" to "18000," it seems logical to assume that Remington was planning to reduce or cease production of the model.

Table 4-A

No. 4 revolver sample frequency for caliber and finish in all serial number intervals.

Caliber					
Serial No. Intervals	Frequency	.38 Rimfire	.38 Centerfire	.41 Rimfire	.41 Centerfire
01 - 2000	42	6	1	32	3
2001 - 4000	26	21		4	1
4001 - 6000	32	29	1		2
6001 - 8000	27	18	6	3	
8001 - 10,000	16			12	4
10,001 - 12,000	16	9	5	2	
12,001 - 14,000	21	10	5	1	5
14,001 - 16,000	9				9
16,001 - 18,000	0				
18,001 - 20,000	22	22			
20,001 - 22,000	27	26	1		
22,001 - 24,000	15	14	1		
TOTAL	253	155	20	54	24
Percentage		61.3%	7.9%	21.3%	9.5%

Finish					
Serial No. Intervals	Frequency	Nickel	Blue	Engraved	Mixed
01 - 2000	42	32	1	6	3
2001 - 4000	26	18		8	
4001 - 6000	32	18	1	13	
6001 - 8000	27	15	1	11	
8001 - 10,000	16	13	1	2	
10,001 - 12,000	16	14	2		
12,001 - 14,000	21	20	1		
14,001 - 16,000	9	8		1	
16,001 - 18,000	0				
18,001 - 20,000	22	22			
20,001 - 22,000	27	27			
22,001 - 24,000	15	14		1	
TOTAL	253	201	7	42	3
Percentage		79.4%	2.8%	16.6%	1.2%

*Not included in this table: Gold finish specimens.

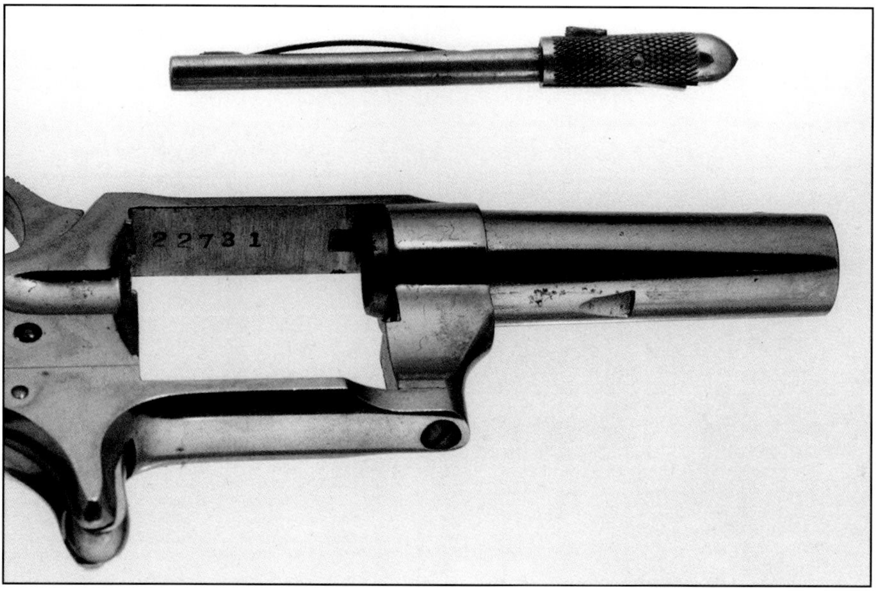

4-01. Detail view of a Remington No. 4 New Model revolver, showing location of serial number under top strap, frame milling under bore projection at cylinder-barrel juncture, shell ejection groove, and spring-retained cylinder center pin.
R.A. Cooper photograph

Serial Number Location and Stamping Practice

Serial number placement for the No. 4 revolver is uniformly located in two places: on the top and bottom straps enclosing the cylinder area (photo 4-01). The cylinder base pin and cylinder must be removed in order to read the number in both locations. Removing the screws retaining both parts of the frame also exposes the numbers.

Contrary to the note in Karr and Karr, no specimen was inspected which bore serial numbers located elsewhere on a standard production revolver.[3] A few pieces have been examined which bear single digits on the grip frame, and occasionally on the back of the cylinder, but these markings have been interpreted as some type of assembly coding, since such specimens also have serial numbers stamped in the usual locations. Serial number "8318" in the Remington Museum is such a specimen (photo 4-02). It appears that the Remington factory did not systematically use an assembly numbering system on parts of the No. 4 revolver.

Only rarely has a specimen been examined without a serial number. These could have been errors, salesmen's samples, factory theft, or a revolver removed from production because of some flaw.

Caliber Data

The 1877 and 1883 Remington Arms Company catalogs showed that the No. 4 revolver was available in .38 and .41 calibers, with five-shot cylinders. But the catalogs do not indicate that the No. 4 was available in those calibers in either rimfire or centerfire. The omission seems to be another lapse in the company's marketing, since Remington had earlier encouraged centerfire selection because of its economy in reloading, especially with the No. 3 revolver. Karr and Karr did indicate that both rimfire and centerfire revolvers were available.[4] Table 4-A portrays the incidence of rimfire and centerfire. The sample data clearly indicates that the most prevalent caliber was .38 rimfire, representing 61.3%, with .41 rimfire representing 21.3% of revolvers extant. It appears that while centerfire cartridges were available, they were not popular during this period of cartridge ignition development. Imperfection in cartridge production resulting in instances of misfire, and a consequent lack of public confidence, were offered as reasons. Records support this, and reveal that .38 centerfire caliber represents 7.5% of the sample, while .41 centerfire makes up 9.5% of the sample.

No specimen was encountered in a caliber other than those mentioned above. Clearly, no regular production run involved calibers other than those cited. There appears to be some serial number grouping for designated calibers, the importance of which cannot be determined. Revolvers in .41 caliber (both rimfire and centerfire) are found between serial numbers "2" through "2586," serial num-

4-02. Remington No. 4 New Model revolver, serial number "8318." Factory engraved in a more ornate pattern than standard, gold plated frame and barrel with the balance nickel plated, imitation "ivory" (celluloid) grips. *Remington Museum collection and photograph*

bers “7442” through “10622,” and serial numbers “13898” through “15549.” No pattern was discerned for .38 caliber specimens, although .38 rimfire sampling is nearly eight times greater than centerfire. Table 4-A reveals additional observations about the calibers produced. The number of specimens in .41 rimfire (fifty-four) is more than double that found in .41 centerfire (twenty-four). Only one interval (“4001” to “6000”) had no sample specimens for .41 rimfire. None were sampled beyond interval “14000.” Intervals “6001” to “8000,” and “10001” to “12000,” contain no sample specimens for .41 centerfire. No specimens were sampled beyond serial number “16000” for .41 centerfire. Considering that less than 10% in both .38 and .41 were sampled for centerfire caliber, it seems safe to assume that cartridge production consistency, quality control, reloading effectiveness, and marketing were important considerations. From interval “18001” to “24000,” only two .38 centerfire specimens have been recorded. All of the remaining sixty-two examples were in .38 rimfire.

Finishes

During this period in firearms manufacturing history, small caliber pistols were generally nickel plated. The nickname “Saturday Night Special” is popularly associated with nickel plated pistols. To the contrary, Remington catalogs showed that blue finish was slightly less expensive than nickel plate. There is some evidence that the nickel plated finish held up to wear better than blue, although nickel plate will exhibit evidence of hard use.

The observed characteristics reveal that 79.4% of the No. 4 revolvers were in plain nickel finish, 2.8% in blued finish, and 16.6% were engraved, usually on nickel plate. With engraved pieces, it was possible to purchase gilt (gold) finished parts (hammer, cylinder, trigger) (photo 4-07), or the entire piece in gold finish. Serial number “8318” in the Remington Museum is another example of a mixed-finish gun, with its frame and barrel in gold and the balance finshed in nickel (photo 4-02).

The Remington catalogs for 1877 and 1883 referred to engraved pieces which were “plated and gilt,” or offered the option of “full plated and engraved.” The gilt finish was apparently offered in two variations, *i.e.*, gold plate and gold wash, the latter a duller and non-reflective finish. Gold wash was clearly the most prevalent variation. Specimens have been examined with parts finished in both types of gold, although the company’s catalogs of the period provided no explanation. Moreover, the catalogs did not detail any other available finishes, such as silver plating. It is entirely possible that a presentation piece might have been finished in silver and gold.

Factory engraving appears in two types of patterns, one having a bit more coverage than the other (photos 4-03, 4-04). Either style apparently was “standard.” Essentially the same motif was applied on either side of the grip frame; in addition, some specimens have slender, wavy lines on the backstrap and the top strap over the cylinder (photo 4-06). A few revolvers have wavy lines on both sides of the barrel, a scroll design on the cylinder, and a star-like pattern on the frame where the barrel is joined (photos 4-03, 4-04). Serial number "8318" (in the Remington Museum) exhibits a considerably more ornate, special engraving design (photo 4-02), whereas the specimens illustrated in photos 4-03 and 4-04 represent typical factory engraving.

There seemed to be no factory policy for grades of engraving, with the exception of "special" or "presentation" revolvers, which were clearly more ornate and distinctive looking (see photo 4-07). Remington catalogs of the period carried no explanation regarding styles of engraving offered, nor were there any photo cuts of engraved revolvers.

It is discerned from Table 4-A that nickel plated finish was the most popular, with 79.4% identified. Only one interval, serial numbers "16001 to "18000,"

4-03. A pair of Remington No. 4 New Model revolvers, showing variations in "standard" factory engraving styles; nickel plated, and fitted with imitation "ivory" (celluloid) grips; left sides. *R.A. Cooper photograph*

lacked a sample specimen. All but one of the other intervals had two-digit entries.

Seven blued specimens, 1.8% of the sample, had only minimal entry per serial number interval, a sample too small on which to make inferences. The majority (four) of the blued specimens were British-proofed, reflecting the English preference for that finish over all others. The blue finish for the No. 4 revolver shows the same low incidence as seen for the Smoot's Patent revolvers.

Forty of the forty-two engraved specimens have four-digit serial numbers, which suggests they were manufactured in the initial history of the No. 4 model. With the exception of serial number "8313" in the Remington Museum, the three mixed-finish specimens recorded were found in interval "1" to "2000," and were the only ones recorded. It cannot be determined why mixed-finish specimens were not sampled in the other intervals. The incidence of engraved specimens (16.6%) and the 1.2% of mixed-finish specimens may have resulted from Remington having limited their production. The decision to produce 79% in nickel plate limited Remington artisans to non-labor intensive work.

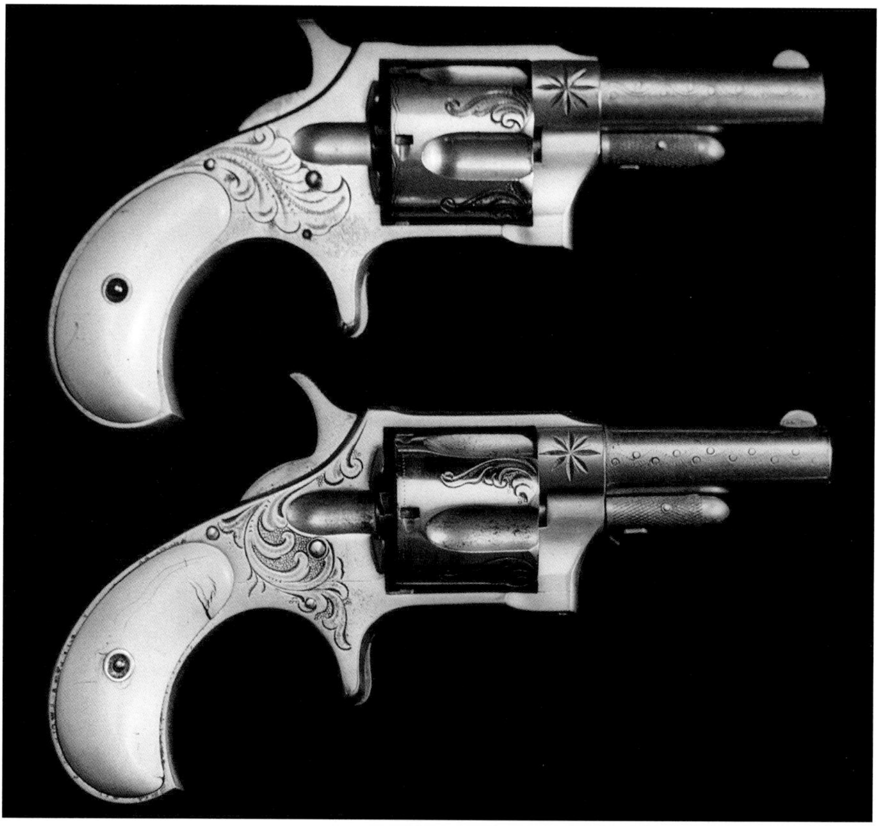

4-04. Right sides of the revolvers illustrated in photo 4-03. *R.A. Cooper photograph*

Forty-two engraved specimens were found in the five initial intervals "1" to "10000," with only two in the intervals "14001" to "18000" and "22001" to "24000." The forty-two specimens represent 16.6% of the sample. No nickel plated specimens were recorded in intervals "16001" to "18000," even though 79.4% of the sample revolvers were finished in nickel.

Types of Grips

The 1877 and 1883 company catalogs indicate that Remington offered ivory, pearl, and checkered hard rubber grips. Oddly, they did not indicate wood, which had proved popular on other Remington models. A review of the descriptive data for other Remington revolvers finds no mention of wood, *per se*. While wood (generally walnut) grips were standard on other Remington arms, examination of specimens of the No. 4 revolver found only five having Remington wood grips (see Table 4-B). Rosewood grips have occasionally been found on other

Table 4-B

No. 4 revolver sample frequency for grip materials in all serial number intervals.

Grip Material									
Serial # Intervals	Freq.	1 Wal.	2 Rose.	3 Pearl	4 Cell.	5 Ivory	6 Chkr. Rubber	7 Sm. Rubber	Unknown
01 - 2000	42		1	5	7	3	13	12	1
2001 - 4000	26				8	2	9	6	1
4001 - 6000	32				9		16	4	3
6001 - 8000	27			2	9	2	14		
8001 - 10000	16			2	1		9	4	
10001 - 12000	16	1			2		11	1	1
12001 - 14000	21		1	1	1		17		1
14001 - 16000	9				1		8		
16001 - 18000	0								
18001 - 20000	22						22		
20001 - 22000	27		2				24	1	
22001 - 24000	15			1	1		13		
TOTAL	253	1	4	11	39	7	156	28	7
Percentage		0.4%	1.6%	4.3%	15.4%	2.8%	61.7%	11.1%	2.8%

1. Walnut 2. Rosewood 3. Pearl 4. Celluloid 5. Ivory 6. Checkered Rubber 7. Smooth Rubber 8. Unknown

Remington pistols, but curiously no explanation was offered in the catalogs about the varieties of wood grips available.

Some comment is in order about the "ivory" grips offered in the Remington catalogs. As discussed in earlier chapters, Remington used a nitrocellulose product called "celluloid" to imitate ivory. On the No. 4 revolver, the size, shape, and color of the "ivory" grips were the same as offered for the Smoot's Patent birdhead grip models. No explanation was found as to why Remington did not inform its customers that the company's "ivory" grip material was in fact an imitation product. It may have been possible to order real ivory, but it was left to the customer to determine its cost and authenticity. Table 4-B reveals that celluloid grips were recorded for thirty-nine specimens, or 15.4%, while genuine ivory was recorded for seven specimens, or 2.8% of the sample.

Black checkered hard rubber grips are most commonly observed on No. 4 revolvers, comprising 61.7%. Smooth black hard rubber grips have also been observed, representing 11.1% of the sample. A few specimens have been examined that were of a dark brown hard rubber, but the incidence was small.

Mother-of-pearl grips were available and one would expect to find them on presentation or engraved No. 4 revolvers. Pearl grips have also been found on nickel plated specimens. Of the engraved pieces examined, 75% had celluloid (imitation ivory) grips. The incidence of pearl grips made up 4.3% of the sample. One explanation for so few revolvers with pearl grips may be related to the cost, which ran 20% more than "ivory."

Hammer

Remington generally case-hardened the hammer and trigger components of its arms. These parts were optionally finished in nickel plate, blue, or gilt to match or complement the balance of the piece. Several production models had only the case-hardened finish exposed. "Specially" engraved pieces had the hammer engraved, although with only a fine, chain-like outline. All hammer spurs have a knurled, or cross-hatched surface.

Trigger

The trigger surfaces were all made in smooth finish. Since the trigger housing exposes little more than the trigger's front surface, no specimens have been observed having any variations.

Springs

Interior springs appear to be quite durable, and remarkably few specimens examined showed any weakness. So few springs contributing to the operation of the revolver provides one reason for their survival rate today. Another factor is the high quality of steel used in this model.

Screws

On all Remington revolver models, screws were soft and easily misshaped by the use of over-size screwdrivers. Because screws were not case-hardened, they were easily ruptured in removal if tightly seated. Screws on all No. 4 revolvers were blued regardless of the balance of the finish of the piece.

Markings

The location of serial numbering was discussed earlier, and it represents the principal marking on Remington No. 4 revolvers. Barrel marking on all production revolvers reads "E. Remington & Sons, Ilion, N.Y." in one $^{1}/_{32}$ inch high line running from the back edge of the front sight to the breech. No variations in type style have been noted. The cylinder was not marked or numbered; neither were the trigger, hammer, cylinder base pin, or other internal parts. Occasionally, a cylinder has been noted marked with a single digit on its back. This could be a type of assembly marking, since serial numbers were present. Serial number "8318" (photo 4-02) is an example of this; it is also marked on the grip frame. Some pieces have been examined with single digits and symbols on interior parts, such as the interior of the recoil shield. Occasionally pieces have been noted with numbers stamped irregularly and with a different numeral font. The significance of these marking variations has not been established, since it involves only a few specimens.

Sights

The front sight is a blade $^{3}/_{32}$ inch high by $^{5}/_{16}$ inch long and recessed into the barrel surface $^{1}/_{32}$ inch back from the muzzle. It is of standard size, finished in nickel plate, and no specimens have been observed with a sight either larger or smaller than the standard dimensions described. The rear sight is an arrow-like notch recessed into the frame immediately above the hammer (photo 4-06).

Barrel and Frame Assembly

No variations in barrel length of the No. 4 revolver were observed, regardless of caliber. All examples have a uniform barrel length of 2½ inches. The No. 4 revolver actually has a significantly shorter barrel than the No. 3 Smoot's Patent revolver, which also was made in .38 caliber.

Cylinder Base Pin: its Removal and Shell Ejection System

The cylinder base pin of the No. 4 revolver represents a departure from the Smoot's Patent revolvers, which utilize the cylinder base pin to house the ejector rod. With the No. 4 revolver, the removal of the base pin serves as the cartridge ejector system. This simple, accessible design made removing the cylinder the means of loading and ejecting cartridges (photo 4-01). Thus, this revolver has no true cartridge ejection system, *i.e.*, an ejector rod. While it may look simplified, the cylinder base pin assembly does represent a source of malfunction in many pieces examined. The pin contains a spring-held button that, when depressed, permits the pin to slide outward from the frame. A milled indentation in the bottom of the barrel engages the spring lever of the cylinder base pin button and prevents the pin from falling out (photo 4-01). The button must be depressed in order to remove the pin and the cylinder. A $^{1}/_{8}$ inch wide flat surface is provided in the length of the cylinder pin head to allow it to slide out from the frame and engage the milled groove in the barrel (photo 4-01).

On all production No. 4 revolvers, the cylinder base pin was case-hardened and then usually nickel plated. Specimens have been observed with the cylinder base pin in blue or gold finish. Although the cylinder base pin head is one inch long by $^{1}/_{4}$ inch thick, and knurled, many specimens have been examined in which a slight bend in the pin (two inches long by $^{5}/_{32}$ inch in diameter) affects the turning of the cylinder. The small spring recessed into the pin was meant to control revolutions, or free spin of the cylinder (photo 4-01). These springs are reasonably sturdy, although if damaged or bent they can affect ease of firing. Any change in the angle of the cylinder base pin head itself readily affects the ease with which it slides out below the barrel, even when the button is fully depressed. This clearly can affect the turning action of the cylinder, the effectiveness of the revolver, and the facility of cartridge ejection.

Bushings

All cylinders have a short, $^{3}/_{32}$ inch bushing in front of the cylinder, and a $^{1}/_{8}$ inch ratchet bushing in the rear which engages a hand or pawl connected to the hammer assembly. Both bushing and ratchet are essentially uniform on all No. 4 revolvers, although some specimens observed show minor variations in size.

Cylinders

While five-shot cylinders were uniform on all No. 4 revolvers, regardless of caliber, some slight variations have been noted. The .41 caliber revolvers appear to have a $1^{1}/_{16}$ inch long cylinder, while the .38 caliber weapons have a $1^{1}/_{8}$ inch long cylinder. This difference appears related to the milling or open space found between the front of the cylinder and the frame (photo 4-01). In some specimens, the front bushing on the cylinder may vary from $^{1}/_{16}$ inch to $^{3}/_{32}$ inch in width. No specimen has been examined having a cylinder without a bushing in the front. All standard production model cylinders have five flutes, and no specimen has been examined without flutes.

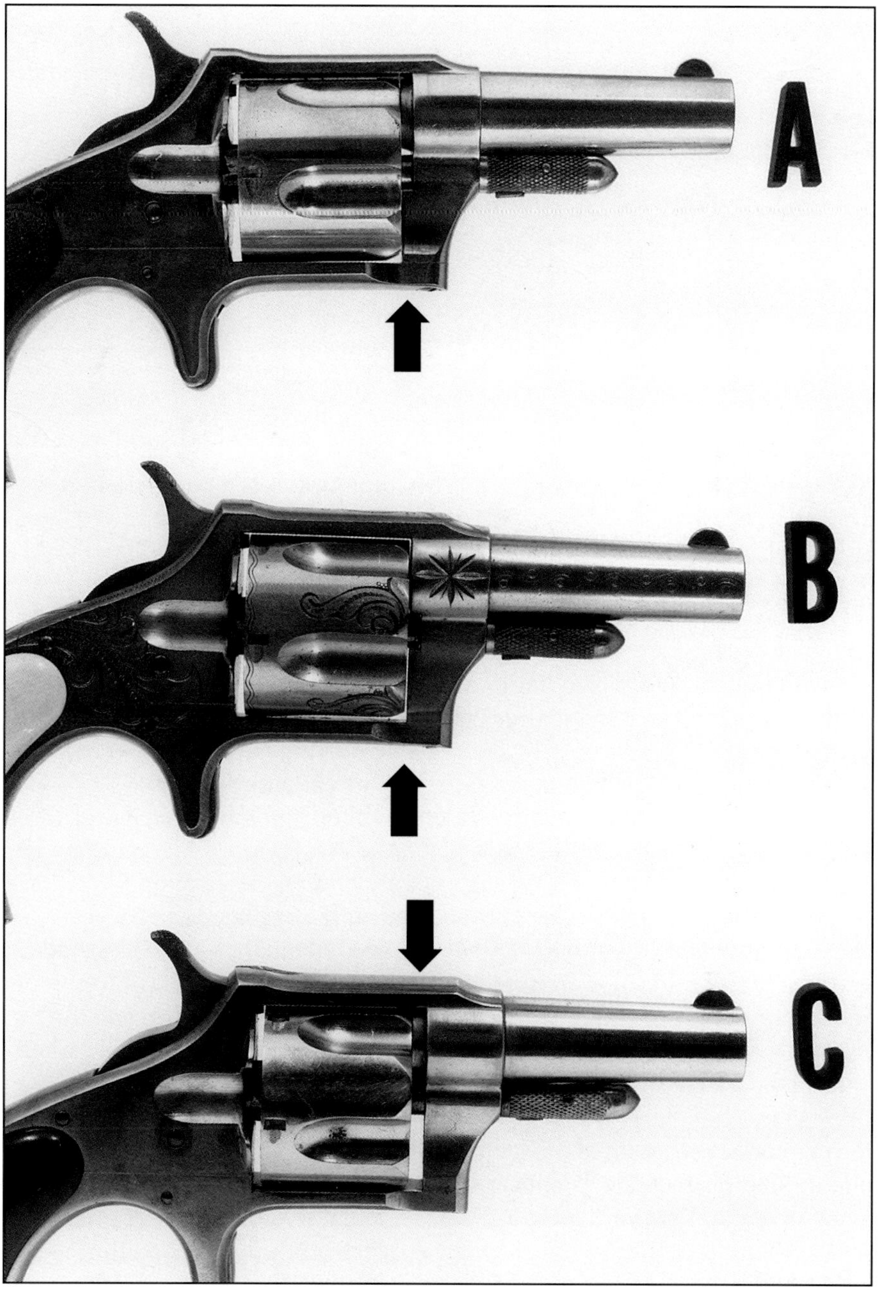

4-05. Detail view of three Remington No. 4 revolvers, showing frame milling variations at cylinder-barrel juncture. "C" illustrates the widest space, as noted on all .41 caliber specimens; "B" illustrates the narrowest space, as noted on factory engraved .38 caliber specimens; "A" illustrates that found in the balance of No. 4 revolver production, without relation to caliber or finish. *R.A. Cooper photograph*

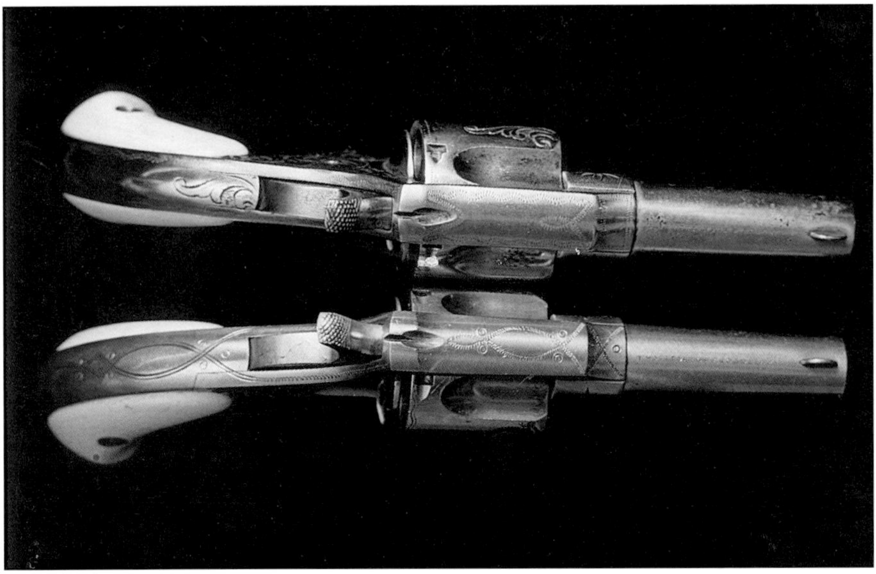

4-06. Top view of two No. 4 New Model revolvers, showing variations in the factory engraving designs and patterns. *R.A. Cooper photograph*

Milling

Three types of frame milling variations (A, B, and C in photo 4-05) are the only ones noted, and each is readily evident. Milling patterns on the No. 4 revolver are apparently related to caliber designation and/or finish, although the significance has not yet been established. All .41 caliber revolvers exhibit the "C" variation, having the most space between the front of the cylinder and the edge of the frame extending from the top to the bottom strap. Particularly evident is the exposure of the barrel projection from the outer surface of the frame. The width of the frame where it joins the barrel is $^{1}/_{16}$ inch more on .41 caliber revolvers. Engraved models in .38 caliber uniformly have the "B" variation. There, what is essentially a notch in the frame for the cylinder bushing exists with no space between the front of the cylinder and the frame. The "A" variation represents the rest of No. 4 revolver production, with no evident relationship to caliber grouping or finish. While milling characteristics appear to bear some relationship to caliber and finish, neither the rationale nor purpose of these milling variations is apparent.

Recoil Shield

All but four of the No. 4 revolvers surveyed for this study had recoil shields of uniform size and shape. On the left side it is arc-like, following the outer lines of the cylinder; the right side is designed for loading with a ½ inch wide opening for shell insertion. An $^{11}/_{16}$ inch long by $^{11}/_{32}$ inch wide flute on the right frame is standard, to facilitate cartridge insertion and ejection (photo 4-04).

Summary

The Remington No. 4 revolver experienced fairly uniform production, with only variations in grips and finish distinguishing one specimen from another. It is estimated that close to 23,000 were manufactured, primarily in .38 caliber. Customers were offered a slightly larger option in .41 caliber. Its symmetry of line, compact snub-nose appearance, and ease of cleaning and assembly, coupled with sturdy construction, place the No. 4 revolver in a class worthy of the Remington Arms Company's notable place in firearms history.

Notes:

1. Harry J. Parker, "Remington Number 4 Revolver, New Model," in *Arms Gazette*, Vol. 1, No. 5, January 1974, p. 34; and "The Remington Number 4 Revolver: Milling Variations," in *Remington Society of America Newsletter*, December 1987, p. 3.
2. Charles L. Karr, Jr. and Carroll R. Karr, *Remington Handguns* (2nd edition), 1951, p. 125.
3. *Ibid.*, p. 125.
4. *Ibid.*, p. 82.

4-07. Remington No. 4 New Model revolver, serial number "1698." Factory engraved, nickel plated with gold washed cylinder, cylinder pin, and hammer, mother-of-pearl grips with "CGC" monogram. Caliber .41 rimfire. Housed in a factory wooden casing with "H" headstamp cartridges and key. *Herb Glass, Jr. collection and photograph*

Table 4-C

Composite of all criteria for the three Smoot Patent and the Number Four revolvers.

	No. 1		No. 2		No. 3			No. 4	
Criteria	Rev. Recoil Shield	Fixed Shield	.30 Caliber	.32 Caliber	BHO	BHR	SH		
Announced Sale in Price List	January 1875	January 1875	0	0	0	0	0	0	
Announced Sale in Dated Catalog	January 1876	January 1876	Oct. 1878	1878	1878	1882	1882	1877	
Lowest Serial Number Recorded	Serial #1	Serial #87	Serial #1	Serial #4	Serial #1005	Serial #15696	Serial #23244	Serial #2	
Highest Serial Number Recorded	Serial #667	Serial #2976	Serial #2090	Serial #2102	Serial #15513	Serial #22111	Serial #27881	Serial #23039	
Estimated Number Produced	3,000		2,000		12,000	7,500	6,000	21,000	
Incidence of Finish									
A. Nickel	66.7%	64.8%	87.2%	71.9%	70.9%	94.4%	79.3%	79.4%	
B. Engraved	31.6%	25.6%	11.5%	24.9%	17.7%	1.8%	17.1%	16.6%	
C. Blue	1.7%	9.6%	1.3%	3.2%	11.3%	1.8%	2.4%	2.8%	
Incidence of Grip Materials									
1. Walnut	26.3%	12.0%	0	3.2%	0	1.8%	3.6%	.4%	
2. Rosewood	33.3%	7.2%	0	.5%	1.6%	0	1.2%	1.6%	
3. Pearl	29.1%	24.8%	6.5%	20.0%	6.4%	1.8%	20.7	4.3%	
4. Celluloid	0	14.4%	6.4%	8.6%	17.7%	7.4%	3.6%	15.4%	
5. Ivory	1.7%	1.6%	0	1.6%	0	1.8%	0	2.8%	
6. Checkered Hard Rubber	8.8%	38.4%	84.6%	65.9%	74.2%	81.5%	65.8%	61.7%	
8. Smooth Hard Rubber	0	.8%	1.3%	0	0	0	0	11.1%	
9. Unknown	1.7%	.8%	1.3%	0	0	5.5%	4.9%	2.8%	
								.38 Cal.	.41 Cal.
Incidence of Rimfire	0	0	0	0	54.8%	100%	76.8%	61.3%	21.3%
Incidence of Centerfire	0	0	0	0	45.2%	0%	23.2%	7.9%	9.5%

Production and sales ceased in 1888 upon receivership.

Epilogue

For over 150 years Remington arms have played a vital role in our nation's history.

One of the company's early enthusiasts was General George Armstrong Custer, who prized the ornately engraved Remington Army Model revolver with his likeness carved on its ivory grips that had been presented by the company. It has been passed down through the generations, and still belongs to the Custer family. Although most U.S. troops stationed in the West used Springfield rifles, several Remington revolvers—likely the personal sidearms used by Custer's officers and men—were later retrieved from the Indians or found along Rosebud Creek following the Battle of Little Big Horn in 1876.

The famed chief of the Chiricahua Apaches, Geronimo, owned a Remington Model 1858 .44 caliber Army revolver that had its barrel shortened from eight inches to 6⅝ inches in length and the factory sight replaced. It may have been captured from a white adversary in battle. Geronimo's Remington, serial number "23214," is now on display at the Southwestern Historical Wax Museum in Dallas, Texas.

Two members of the notorious Jesse James gang—Jesse's brother Frank, and Cole Younger—likewise preferred Remington handguns. When Frank James surrended to Missouri Governor Thomas T. Crittenden on October 5th, 1882, he handed over his Remington revolver with the words, "Governor, for the first time in twenty-one years I now permit another man to take my pistol." Frank James' gun was a .44-40 caliber, nickel-plated Model 1875 Single-Action, serial number "15116."

In his book, *Shots Fired in Anger*, author Robert Elman relates how in 1943 then-Lt. General George S. Patton wrote from Sicily requesting relatives to send him a Remington .380 caliber Model 51 semi-automatic pistol. Although the Model 51 had been out of production since 1935, Major General Kenyon A. Joyce contacted Roy Swan at Remington, who located a used one, had it reconditioned and inscribed on the backstrap, and shipped it overseas along with a supply of ammunition. General Patton's Model 51 pistol is serial number "PA-15470," with a 3½ inch barrel; he replaced its original hard rubber grips with ones made of walnut having three stars inlaid on the right side. Later he added a fourth star after being promoted to full general. Today it is on display at the West Point Museum.

WILLIAM S. SMOOT. 2 Sheets—Sheet 1.

Improvement in Breech-loading Fire-arms.

No. 120,788. Patented Nov. 7, 1871.

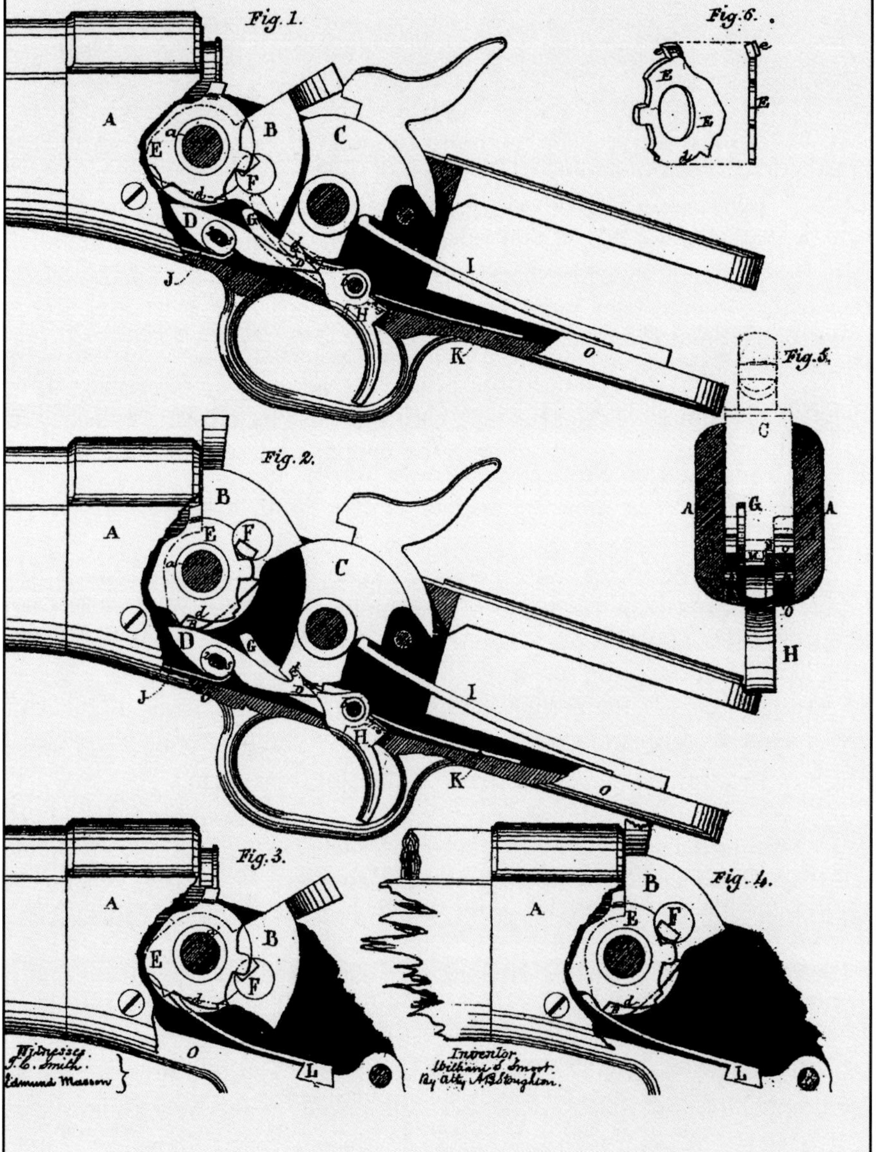

Appendix

The Firearms Patents of William Sydney Smoot while employed by the Remington Arms Company

No. 116,105 **Improvement in Metallic Cartridges.** June 20, 1871
Method of reducing the cost of manufacturing reloadable centerfire metallic cartridges, by riveting a base of iron or other less expensive metal onto a flange on the copper case.

No. 116,106 **Improvement in Breech-Loading Fire-Arms.** June 20, 1871
Places at the open barrel breech of a gun a pivoting solid steel breechblock operated by action of the hammer, that rotates back to permit loading in the manner of the Remington Rolling-Block action. The design also included an automatic ejector.

No. 120,338 **Improvement in Metallic Cartridges.** October 24, 1871
Method of strengthening the head of a cartridge case by pressing a disk of lead, zinc or other malleable metal through the copper case and into the head. The process was done without heating or melting the reinforcing metal disk, and thus was made cheaper.

No. 120,788 **Improvement in Breech-loading Fire-Arms.** November 7, 1871
Improvement to the Remington Rolling-Block action, by which the breech was mechanically locked in the closed position and the hammer left in safety position. The cartridge extractor mechanism also was improved.

No. 133,063 **Improvement in Breech-Loading Fire-Arms.** November 12, 1872
Improvement to the Remington Rolling-Block action, by which the breechblock was locked closed and the firing pin was withdrawn into the breechblock on opening the breech for loading.

No. 143,855 **Improvement in Revolving Fire-Arms.** October 21, 1873
Improvement in the design of small-frame revolvers, by which the barrel and frame were made of one piece of metal; also covered the unique designs of the revolving recoil shield, the center pin, and integral ejector rod.

W. S. SMOOT.

Cartridges for Fire-Arms.

No. 152,428. Patented June 23, 1874.

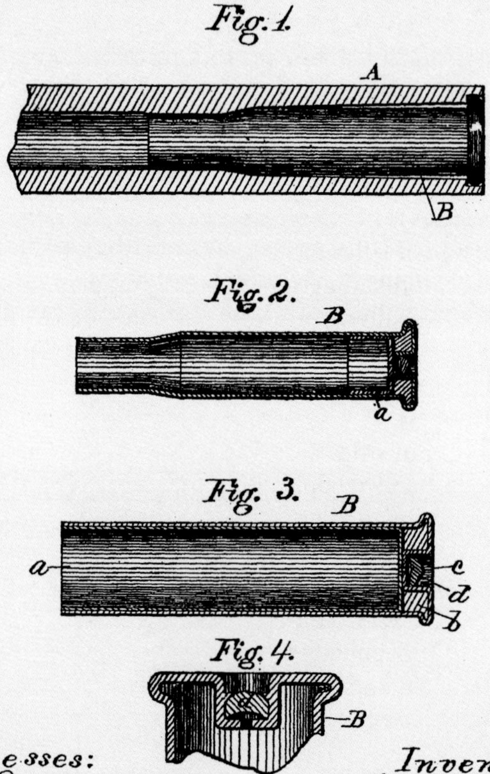

Witnesses:
W. W. Dodge
Jno. D. Patten

Inventor:
W. S. Smoot
by Dodge & Son
Attys

No. 152,428 **Improvement in Cartridges for Fire-Arms.** June 23, 1874
Method of reinforcing the head of a cartridge by pressing a soft metal disk into it causing the disk to expand and fill the cavity, and for securing the anvil in the primer cup; also the design for a tapered barrel chamber to form an effective gas seal and permit easy extraction.

No. 170,780 **Improvement in Primers for Cartridges.** December 7, 1875
Improvement in the design of reloadable metallic cartridges, whereby the primer was made more simply and cheaply using an anvil cut from wire, and by crimping the primer edge to retain the anvil in place.

No. 178,683 **Improvement in Cartridges.** June 13, 1876
Method of forming the base of the anvil within a cartridge case head to retain the anvil in place while allowing flame from the primer to pass by it on the sides, thus causing ignition.

No. 7,827 **Improvement in Magazine Fire-Arms.**
(Division A) Reissued July 31, 1877
Improvement in the design of rifles having under-barrel tube cartridge magazines, pivoting cartridge lifters, and sliding bolts with internal firing pins, whereby the breech is held closed by the sliding bolt having an annular locking lobe.

No. 7,828 **Improvement in Magazine Fire-Arms.**
(Division B) Reissued July 31, 1877
Improvement in the design of rifles as above, whereby cartridges are pushed onto the lifter by spring action and retained within the receiver when lifted into the chamber; and having a mechanism permitting single-shot operation.

No. 196,545 **Design for a Cartridge-Loading Machine.** October 30, 1877
(Granted to W.S. Smoot and Henry H. Hamilton)
Among the numerous improvements claimed were: Automatic handling of cartridge cases, bullets, powder, and primers; automatic die-sizing of cases and bullets; visual and bell indicators for low powder supply; and fully automated loading.

No. 255,822 **Improvement to Primer for Cartridges.** April 4, 1882
Method for manufacturing metallic cartridge primers to insure more dependable ignition, thus preventing misfires or "hang-fires." Accomplished by the use of an anvil so shaped to receive the firing pin at any angle, and having a central aperture for the priming flame to pass directly through to the powder charge.

The listing of W.S. Smoot's patents presented above is complete to the best of the authors' knowledge, but it should not be taken as absolutely comprehensive.

3 Sheets—Sheet 1.

W. S. SMOOT & H. H. HAMILTON.

Cartridge-Loading Machine.

No. 196,545 Patented Oct. 30, 1877.

Fig. 1.

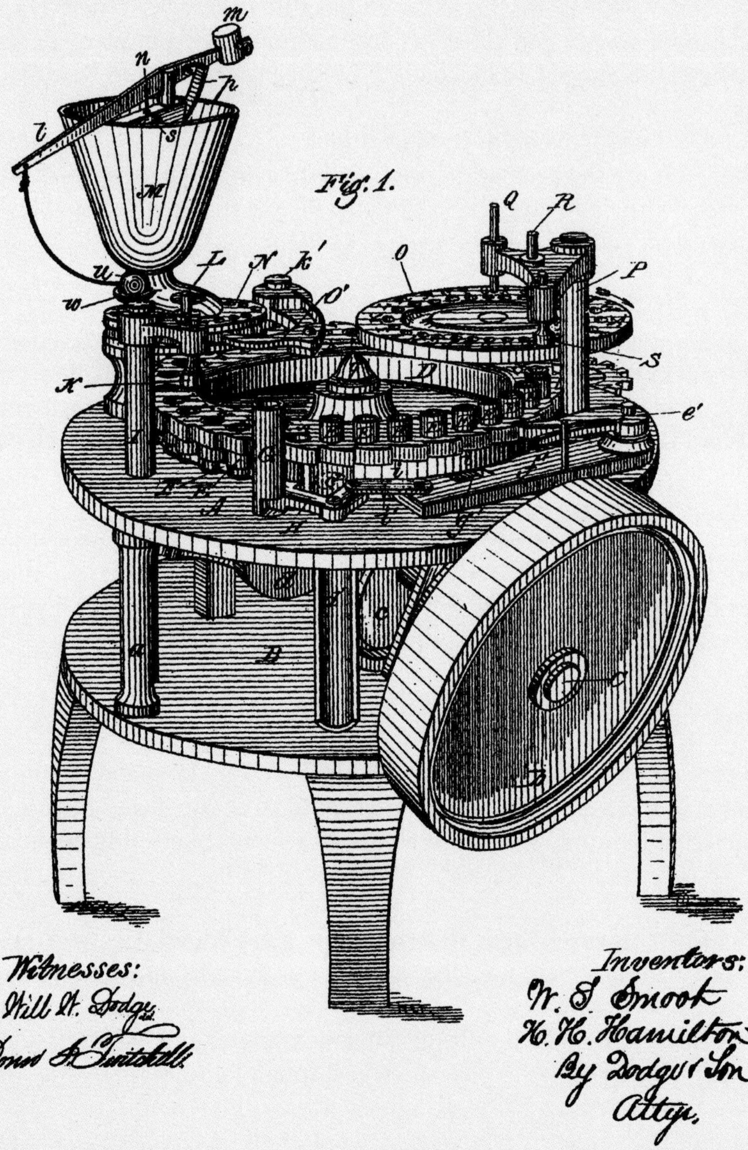

Witnesses:
Will A. Dodge
Dono A. Teitchell

Inventors:
W. S. Smoot
H. H. Hamilton.
By Dodge & Son.
Attys.

Bibliography

Robert W.D. Ball, *Remington Firearms, The Golden Age of Collecting*. Iola, WI: Krause Publications, 1995.

Ella Dimmock, *Ilion History,* Volumes I and II. Unpublished manuscript, undated.

Robert Elman, *Shots Fired in Anger*. New York, NY: Doubleday, 1968.

Alden Hatch, *Remington Arms in American History*. New York, NY: Rinehart and Company, 1956.

Francis B. Heitman, *Historical Register and Dictionary of the United States Army*, Volume I. Washington, DC: Government Printing Office, 1903.

Albert B. Iardella, *Western Electric and the Bell System, a Survey of Service*. New York, NY: Western Electric Company, 1964.

Charles L. and Carroll R. Karr, *Remington Handguns* (2nd edition). Harrisburg, PA: Stackpole Books, 1951.

Jerry Landskron, *Remington Rolling Block Pistols*. Buena Park, CA: Rolling Block Press, 1981.

Howard M. Madaus, Simon Stoddard and Paul Goodwin, *The Guns of Remington*. Dayton, KY: Biplane Productions, 1997.

Roy M. Marcot, *Remington, America's Oldest Gunmaker*. Ilion, NY: Remington Arms Company, 1998.

G. Noether, *Introduction to Statistics, a Fresh Approach*. Boston, MA: Houghton-Mifflin Co., 1971.

Harry J. Parker, "Remington No. 2 Revolver," in *Third Annual Wisconsin Gun Collector*, Wisconsin Gun Collectors Association, Inc., 1964.

_____, Personal Communication with Remington authority Karl F. Moldenhauer, 1970.

_____, "Remington Number 4 Revolver, New Model (Smoot's Patent)," in *Arms Gazette*, Vol. 1, No. 5, January 1974.

_____, "Remington Number 3 Revolver, New Model," in *Arms Gazette*, Vol. 2, No. 4, December 1974.

_____, "Remington Number 1 Revolver, New Model (Smoot's Patent)," in *Arms Gazette*, Vol. 2, No. 11, July 1975.

_____, "Remington Number 2 Revolver, New Model (Smoot's Patent), Part I," in *Arms Gazette*, Vol. 3, No. 7, March 1976.

_____, "Remington Number 2 Revolver, New Model (Smoot's Patent), Part II," in *Arms Gazette*, Vol. 3, No. 8, April 1976.

_____ and Joan S. Reisch, "Three Remington Smoot Revolvers, Serial Numbering and Production Estimates," in *Man at Arms*, Vol. 5, No. 4, July/August 1983.

_____, "The Remington Number 4 Revolver: Milling Variations," in *Remington Society of America Newsletter*, December 1987.

_____, "The Remington Number 1 New Model (Smoot's Patent): Revolving Recoil Shield, Numbering, Cylinder, and Ejector Rod," in *Remington Society of America Newsletter*, September 1988.

_____, "Celluloid Grips for Smoot's Patent and Number 4 Revolvers," in *Remington Society of America Newsletter*, June 1990.

_____ and Joan S. Reisch, "Three Remington Revolvers (Smoot's Patent) Serial Numbers and Production," in *Man at Arms*, Vol. 16, No. 6, November/December 1994.

Harold L. Peterson, *The Remington Historical Treasury of American Guns*. New York, NY: Thomas Nelson & Sons, 1966.

Public Auction of the Karl F. Moldenhauer Collection of Remington Arms. Hyannis, MA: Richard A. Bourne Co., 1980.

Remington Arms Co. Catalogs, Price Lists, and Brochures, various issues 1874-1884. Ilion, NY: Remington Arms Company.

Remington Arms Co. Sole Agents' Catalogs, 1885, 1886, and 1887 issues. Ilion, NY: Remington Arms Company.

W.J. Roff and J.R. Scott, *Handbook of Common Polymers*. London, England: Butterworth, Publisher, 1971.

A.N. Russell, "Ilion and the Remingtons," Paper Presented at the Herkimer County Historical Society, September 1897. Herkimer, NY: Citizen Publishing Company, 1897.

Warren E. Schulz, *Ilion—The Town Remington Made.* Hicksville, NY: Exposition Press, 1977.

Arthur T. Smith, Papers Read Before the Herkimer County Historical Society 1896-1898. Herkimer, NY: Citizen Publishing Company, 1899.

James R. Somers, "The Remington New Line Revolvers," in *The Texas Gun Collector*, Vol. 59, June 1955.

_____, "Letter to the Editor," in *The Texas Gun Collector*, Vol. 64, November 1955.

Bill West, *Remington Arms and History* (2nd edition). Glendora, CA: The author, 1988.

Jerrald H. Zar, *Biostatistical Analysis* (4th edition). Saddle River, NJ: Prentice Hall, 1999.

Acknowledgments

To be a co-author is the height of a relationship, acknowledgment in the broadest sense. To attempt to enumerate the qualities for the public's attention may not be easily identified or unique. Acknowledgment of co-authors in this case is particularly complex, because the second author is a long-term spouse and the third author a long-time academic colleague. In both cases the relationships surround writing and publication activity with the senior author; as distinguished in this volume it is seen as a collective "last hurrah!"

Starting with a collegial relationship as a medical center photographer, **Robert Cooper** (Sequim, WA) twenty-five years later has provided his consent to re-use his photographs for the majority of the photographic illustrations found in this volume. His affirmative response meant a wider set of viewers would have the pleasure of seeing his award-winning photography.

Creating a book format goes beyond journal manuscripts and now calls for computer facility and word-processing sophistication. We were fortunate to have **Marty Martin** of Dallas, Texas, who is a consultant and office manager for a professional association. That tells it all! Her deft preparation of tabular-numeric data added to the impact of the material and yields a graphic dimension.

We are especially grateful for the reading of the manuscript by two Remington arms authorities who are past presidents of the Remington Society of America (RSA): **Fritz Baehr** and **Gordon Stanley**. Both offered suggestions and options for the treatment of the text and the tabular presentations. **Wallace Beinfeld**, former editor of *Arms Gazette*, consented to read the manuscript after seeing it twenty-five years previously as separate magazine articles on the four models.

We are truly indebted to several prominent Remington collectors-writers for elements reflecting their expertise. **Roy Marcot**, **Edward Hull**, **F. Jay Huber**, and **Leon Wier, Jr.** all have places in the pantheon of Remington arms history and research. They have cooperated with the senior author over the years, giving tips, hints, and data sources. Their collective stimulus is imbedded in this writing.

For the senior author, singular inspiration came from **James R. Somers**, in his pioneer article printed in *The Texas Gun Collector* in 1955. Mr. Somers' was the only prior publication on Smoot's Patent and No. 4 revolvers, and represents the legacy followed to the development of this volume. Following the old oak tree adage, this small magazine article maintained its power for over forty years.

Also over the years, early contacts with various **Remington Company** officials in Ilion, New York, and specifically at the **Remington Museum**, provided a base of information threaded into this volume. Innumerable gun dealers and collectors at antique gun shows nationwide were contributors to data collection, and their generally consistent consent to inspect weapons and record data forms the axis of this book.

We are pleased that the editors of *Man at Arms*, *Arms Gazette*, and *Remington Society Newsletter/Journal* granted permission to use prior writings of the senior author and his associates. It is these earlier publications that readily became the basis for this volume. We are heartened by their collective affirmative response.

Of **Richard G. Gooding** of Dallas, Texas, much can be said, for he was an early Remington collector and a repository of information. He has aided and abetted the senior author's collecting and knowledge base, earlier in the Midwest and later in the Southwest, for many decades.

Casting a tall shadow over this volume is the memory of **Karl F. Moldenhauer**. Karl was both visible and discursive, usually on Remington subjects in social circles. He had the capacity to produce dialogue that stimulated research and is now belatedly appreciated. Karl's legacy is found in his collection catalog, and in the many exchanges of personal correspondence with the senior author. Both his footprints and his shadow are found throughout these pages.

For long and tedious research in old newspapers, files, and other sources, we are grateful to staff members at the Ilion (New York) Free Public Library: **Christine Lozoski**, **Joan M. Stalloch**, and Historian **Michael Disotelle**.

To the **Mooney** family: **Sara**, **Brandon**, and **Andrew**. We marvel at their facility to initiate computer searches.

We were particularly rewarded by the response of **Barbara A. Sweeney**, Assistant Staff Manager of the AT&T Archives, who provided the portrait and obituary of William S. Smoot.

The expertise of **Karen Kaiser** with computer data sources was notable. That, coupled with her professional experience in providing genealogy services for the Sherman, Texas Public Library, make her contribution to this volume unique.

Finally, we wish to recognize the professional cooperation of **Paul Goodwin**, noted arms photographer, for providing us with eleven photographs from Madaus, Stoddard and Goodwin's *The Guns of Remington* volume. These photos were chosen to highlight the engraving and finish variations not present in the text photographs of the four featured revolver models.

Index

A

American Bell Telephone Co. ....vii, ix
Appomattox Court House, VA xv
Army of Northern Virginia..xv

B

Bangs (Smoot), Mary.........viii
Barrels ......*see chapter discussions*
Barton, Enos..................viii-ix
Beals, Fordyce.....................17
Boston, MA...............viii, x-xi
Bridgeport, CT............xiii, xvi
Brookline, MA...................viii
Bushings ......*see chapter discussions*

C

Calibers ......*see chapter discussions*
Cartridges ......*see chapter discussions*
Catalogs, Remington arms...... 19-22, 27, 29-33, 53, 58-59, 62, 66-68, 71-74, 76, 81, 85, 88-90, 92-93, 97-99, 101
Centerfire .....*see Calibers/Cartridges*
Chamberlain Trap & Target Co.......................xvi
Chestertown, MD...............xvi
Chicago, IL..............ix, 19, 93
Chiricahua Apaches...........109
Cincinnati, OH...................xiv
Civil War......vii-ix, xiv-xv, 17
Clayton, Dubilier & Rice...xvi
Cleveland, OH....................viii
Clough, J.W........................viii
Colt's Patent Fire Arms Mfg. Co.......................xv, 17, 19
Congressional Globe...........vii
Congressional Record.........vii
Crane's Corners, NY..........xiii
Crittenden, MO Governor Thomas T. 109
Custer, Gen. George Armstrong....................109
Cylinder Pins ......*see chapter discussions*
Cylinders ......*see chapter discussions*

D

Deringer, Henry.......xv, 17, 19
Dun Report....................viii-ix
DuPont, de Nemours & Co., E.I.................................xvi
DuPont, Samuel Francis.....vii

E

Ejector Rods ......*see chapter discussions*
Elliot, William.....................17
Engraving...21, 25, 29-32, 58-62, 73-75, 83, 89, 98-102
E. Remington & Sons..vii-xvi, 17, 29, 67
"*E. Remington & Sons, Ilion, N.Y.*" barrel marking....103
"*E. Remington & Sons, Ilion, N.Y., Pat. W.S. Smoot, Oct. 21, 1873*" barrel marking ... .36, 76
Erie River...........................17
Evanston, IL.........................ix

F

Federal Act of 1855............vii
Finishes ......*see chapter discussions*
First Maryland Infantry......vii
Frames ......*see chapter discussions*
Furniture, Gun...................xiii

G

Geronimo, Apache Chief...109
Grant, Gen. Ulysses S.........xv
Gray, Elisha........................viii
Griffiths, John.....................xiv
Grips—styles/materials ......*see chapter discussions*

H

Hammers ......*see chapter discussions*
Harpers Ferry, VA Armory/Arsenal......xiii-xiv
Hartley & Graham..............xvi
Hyatt, J.W. (chemist)...........32

I

Ilion, NY.....xi, xiv-xvi, 17, 67
Ilion, NY *Citizen*.............ix-xi
Ilion, NY Rifle Club............xi

J

James, Jesse.......................109
James, Frank......................109
Jenks carbines.....................xiv
Joyce, Gen. Kenyon A.......109

L

Lamberson Co.....................19
Lamberson, Furman & Co. 19, 93
Lawrence, D.H. 93
Lee, Gen. Robert E..............xv
Liége, Belgium...................xiii
Litchfield, NY....................xiii
Little Big Horn, Battle of..109
London, England................xiii

M

Madison, NC......................xvi
Manifest Destiny.................xv
Markings ......*see chapter discussions*
Mayfield, KY.................... xvi
Maynard tape primers........xiv
Mexican War.................xiv-xv

Milling
......*see chapter discussions*
Mississippi Rifles, U.S.
Model 1841....................xiv
Mohawk River....................xiv

N

Naval Efficiency Board.......vii
New York, NY..............19, 93
Norfolk, VA.........................vii

O

Oberlin College.................viii

P

Paris, France.......................xiii
Parker Shotgun Co. xvi
Patents............19-20, 110-114
Patton, Gen. George S.......109
Peters Cartridge Co. xvi
Production of Models
......*see chapter discussions*
Proof Marks, British..........100

R

Recoil Shields
Fixed (FS)
Revolving (RRS)
......*see chapter discussions*
Remington Arms
Army Model .44 cal.
revolver.............17, 109
Double Derringer pistol..19
Elliot's Ring-Trigger
pistol..........................17
Hepburn rifle 17
Lee magazine rifle..........17
Model 1875 .44-40 cal.
Single-Action revolver
.................................109
Model 51 .380 cal.
Semi-Auto pistol 109
Navy Model .36 cal.
revolver.....................17
New Line revolver/
markings........19, 67, 93
New Model Belt revolver
...................................17
New Model Pocket
revolver 17, 67, 85,
91-107
New Model Police revolver
...................................17
No. 1 Smoot Patent
revolver....17-53, 57-59,
62, 64-66, 68, 75, 77-79
No. 2 Smoot Patent
revolver ..21, 30, 39, 45,
51-66, 68, 75, 77-79
No. 3 Smoot Patent
revolver 21, 27-28,
30, 35, 46-48, 51, 53,
67-92, 97, 103
No. 4 New Model revolver
...19, 21, 27, 30, 35, 48,
51, 53, 64, 73, 92-107
Revolving rifle...............17
Rider's Vest-Pocket pistol
.............................17, 29
Rolling-Block rifle 17
Split-Breech pistol..........17
Sporting rifle................109
Walking-Cane rifle 17
Remington Arms Co....vii-xvi,
17-19, 20-22, 25, 27-29,
33, 50, 53-54, 60, 62, 64-
65, 67, 69, 71, 73, 75-76,
83, 85-86, 90-94, 96-97,
100-103, 107, 109
Remington Arms Museum ......
.............53, 58, 96, 98-100
Remington, Eliphalet II
("Lite") ....xii-xiv
Remington, Eliphalet, III ....
.................................xiv-xv
Remington Farms..............xvi
Remington, Philo ....xiv-xv
Remington Rand xvi
Remington, Samuel.......xiv-xv
Remington-UMC................xvi
Rider, Joseph 17
Rifling
......*see chapter discussions*
Rimfire
.....*see Calibers/Cartridges*
Rosebud Creek 109

S

Sabine River xv
"Saturday Night Special"
revolvers..................72, 98
Screws
......*see chapter discussions*
Serial Numbers
......*see chapter discussions*
Sharps Rifle Co. ....xv, 17
Shawk, George viii
Sights *see chapter discussions*
Smoot, Anna T. viii
Charles H. viii
Joseph E.......................viii
Joseph E., Capt. vii
Margaret.......................viii
Mary.............................viii
Mary Bangs viii
Sarah M. viii
William Sydney ....vi-xi,
xvi, 19, 49, 52
W.S., Jr.........................viii
Southwestern Historical Wax
Museum........................109
Spencer Rifle Co. xv
Sperry Rand........................xvi
Springfield, MA
Armory/Arsenal.....viii, xiii
Rifle.............................109
Springs
......*see chapter discussions*
Stager, Gen. Anson ....viii-ix
Stanton, U.S. Sect'y. of War
Edwin M. xiv
Stocks ....*see Grips*
Suffolk County, MA..............x
Swan, Roy (Remington Arms
Co.)..............................109

T

Triggers
......*see chapter discussions*
Typewriters, Remington ....
.................................ix, xvi

U

Union Metallic Cartridge Co.
................................xvi, 17
U.S. Express Co. 90
U.S. Military Telegraphers..viii
U.S. Navy vii
U.S. Ordnance Dept. vii
U.S. Patent Office xi
Utica, NY xiii

W

Washington, D.C............vii, x
West Point Museum 109
Western Electric Co. ....vii-x
World War I.......................xvi
Armistice.......................xvi
World War II......................xvi

Y

Younger, Cole...................109